Shirley Valent...
One for the R...

'Shirley Bradshaw, née Valentine, ...
literally wedded to the home, tied to having Joe's tea on the table, a
"St Joan of the Fitted Units" . . . But Shirley's journey from resigned
fatalism to fulfilled self-discovery is a joy.'

Robin Thornber, *Guardian*

One for the Road 'starts . . . with the mid-life hero torn between the
security of married life in a dormer bungalow on a northern housing
estate and dreams of being a rucksacked super-tramp. Mr Russell
writes with knowledgeable venom about a world where Beethoven
Underpass leads to Wagner Walkway and where anyone who doesn't
join Weight Watchers or the Ramblers Club is regarded as a social
deviant.'

Francis King, *Sunday Telegraph*

WILLY RUSSELL was born in Whiston near Liverpool and left
school at fifteen. He went through a succession of jobs before, at the
age of twenty, he decided to take 'O' and 'A' levels and become a
teacher. At about the same time he saw John McGrath's play *Unruly
Elements* at the Everyman Theatre, Liverpool, and decided he wanted
to become a playwright. Since then he has written *Blind Scouse*
(Edinburgh Festival, 1972), *John Paul George Ringo . . . and Bert*
(Everyman; Lyric Theatre, London; winner of the Evening Standard's
and the London Theatre Critics' award for Best Musical, 1974),
Breezeblock Park (Everyman; Mermaid, London, 1975), *One for the
Road* (Contact Theatre, Manchester, 1986, on tour, 1978, revised for
Lyric Theatre, London, 1988), *Stags & Hens* (Liverpool Playhouse,
1978) and *Educating Rita* (RSC Warehouse; Piccadilly Theatre, 1980;
RSC tour, 1982; winner of the Society of West End Theatres' award
for Best Comedy in 1980; made into a film, for which Russell wrote
the screenplay, directed by Lewis Gilbert and starring Michael Caine
and Julie Walters, in 1983). The musical *Blood Brothers* (Liverpool
Playhouse; Lyric Theatre, London, 1983) for which he wrote the
music and lyrics as well as the book. *Shirley Valentine* (Everyman,
Liverpool, 1986; screenplay, 1987; Vaudeville Theatre, London,
1988). His television work includes *King of the Castle* (BBC 'Second
City Firsts', 1973), *Break-In* (BBC TV play for schools, 1974), *Death
of a Young Man* (BBC 'Play for Today', 1974), *Our Day Out* (BBC
'Play for Today', 1976; subsequently adapted for the stage and seen
at the Everyman, Liverpool, in 1983), and *The Daughters of Albion*
(Yorkshire TV, 1978). In June 1983 the Open University awarded him
an Honorary M.A. in recognition of his work as a playwright.

by the same author

EDUCATING RITA, STAGS & HENS
   AND BLOOD BROTHERS
OUR DAY OUT

The photograph on the front cover shows Pauline Collins as Shirley
Valentine *at the Vaudeville Theatre, London (photo: Catherine
Ashmore). The back cover photograph of Willy Russell is by Phil
Cutts.*

WILLY RUSSELL

Shirley Valentine and One for the Road

METHUEN DRAMA

A METHUEN PAPERBACK

This collection first published as a paperback original in Great
Britain in 1988 by Methuen Drama, Michelin House, 81 Fulham
Road, London SW3 6RB and distributed in the United States of
America by HEB Inc., 70 Court Street, Portsmouth, New
Hampshire 03801, USA.

Reprinted 1989

British Library Cataloguing in Publication Data

Russell, Willy
   Shirley Valentine : including Shirley
   Valentine & One for the road.—(Methuen
   modern play).
   I. Title
   822′.914

   ISBN 0-413-89503-3

Set in 9pt Plantin by 🅰Tek Art Ltd., Croydon, Surrey
Printed in Great Britain by
Cox & Wyman Ltd, Reading

Shirley Valentine

Shirley Valentine was first performed at the Everyman Theatre, Liverpool on 13 March 1986. The part of Shirley Valentine was played by Noreen Kershaw. The director was Glen Walford, designer Claire Lyth and the lighting was by Brian Harris.

Shirley Valentine was subsequently produced in London at the Vaudeville Theatre on 21 January 1988 and won the Lawrence Olivier Award for Comedy of the Year 1988. The part of Shirley Valentine was played by Pauline Collins. The director was Simon Callow, designer Bruno Santini and the lighting was by Nick Chelton.

ACT ONE

Scene One

The kitchen of a semi-detached house. It is a well-established kitchen, bearing signs of additions and alterations which have been made over the years. It is not a highly personalised palace of pitch pine and hanging baskets but nevertheless has signs of personality having overcome the bleakness of the chipboard and formica . . . It is quite a comfortable and reassuring place.

Specifically the kitchen contains (apart from the obvious cooker, fridge, etc.) a door which leads out of the house, a wall with a window, a dining table and chairs.

As we open, SHIRLEY is beginning preparations for cooking the evening meal – this includes opening a bottle of white wine from which she pours a glass. Throughout the following scene she sets a table for two and she prepares, cooks and finally serves one of the truly great but unsung dishes of the world – chips and egg.

SHIRLEY. Y'know I like a glass of wine when I'm doin' the cookin'. Don't I wall? Don't I like a glass of wine when I'm preparing the evenin' meal. Chips an' egg! (*Takes a sip of wine.*) I never used to drink wine. It was our Millandra who started me on this. She said to me, she said 'Mother! Mother, nobody drinks rum an' coke these days. Everybody drinks wine now. Oh Mother have a glass of Riesling instead.' Kids. They know everything don't they? Our Millandra was goin' through her slightly intellectual phase at the time. Y'know her, an' her mate – Sharron-Louise. Because it was all white wine an' Bruce Springsteen at the time. Y' know the pair of them stopped goin' down the clubs in town an' started hangin' out in that Bistro all the time. Y' know where the artists go. They seen, erm, what's his name one night, erm Henry Adrian, yeh. Apparently Sharron-Louise got his autograph. And breakfast as well I believe. Anyway, the pair of them are out of that phase now. And am I glad? Because y' know the two of them'd sit at the table for hours an' all's y'd hear from the pair of them was: 'It

was great. It was great. Was a laugh wasn't it?' Then they'd
both go back into trance for half an hour an' you'd suddenly
hear: 'It was brilliant last night. It was more than brilliant. It
was mega brill.' 'Yeh it was, it was double fab wasn't it?' And
d' y' know, no matter how long they sat there, you'd never get
to know what it was that was so double fab an' mega brill.
(*Pause.*) Maybe it was the breakfasts! Mind you I do miss them,
the kids. Our Millandra shares a flat with Sharron-Louise now.
An' our Brian's livin' in a squat. In Kirkby. I said to him, I
said, 'Brian, if you're gonna live in a squat, son, couldn't y'
pick somewhere nice. Y know somewhere like Childwall?'
'Mother,' he said to me. 'Childwall is no place for a poet.' 'Cos
that's our Brian's latest scheme y' see. He's always got a
scheme. This one is – he's become Britain's first ever busker
poet. What's he like wall? The language. 'I hate the fuckin'
daffodils/I hate the blue remembered hills.' He's loop the loop.
Mind you, I'm glad he's given up archery. Oh God, look at the
time. What am I doin' sitting' here talkin' and 'he'll' be in for
his tea won't he. An' what's he like? My Feller. What's he like
wall? Well he likes everything to be as it's always been. Like his
tea always has to be on the table as he comes through that
door. If the plate isn't landin' on the table just as his foot is
landin' on the mat, there's ructions. I've given up arguin'. I
said to him, once, I said, 'Listen Joe, if your tea isn't on the
table at the same time every night it doesn't mean that the
pound's collapsed y' know, or that there's been a world disaster.
All it means Joe, is that one of the billions of human bein's on
this planet has to eat his tea at a different time.' Well did it do
any good? I could've been talkin' to that. Couldn't I wall, I
could've been talkin' to you. (*Pause.*) I always said I'd leave
him when the kids grew up – but by the time they'd grown up
there was nowhere to go. Well you don't start again at forty-two
do y'? They say don't they, they say once you've reached your
forties life gets a bit jaded an' y' start to believe that the only
good things are things in the past. Well I must have been an
early developer; I felt like that at twenty-five. I'm not sayin'
he's bad, my feller. He's just so bleedin' good. Mind you, I
think most of them are the same aren't they? I mean they're
lovely at first. Y' know when they're courtin' y'. Y' know before

you've had the horizontal party with them, oh they're
marvellous then. They'll do anything for y'. Nothin' is too much
trouble. But the minute, the very minute after they've first had
y' – their behaviour starts to change. It's like that advert isn't
it? I was watchin' it the other night – y' know, Milk Tray Man.
Oh he's marvellous isn't he? Y' see him, he dives off a
thousand-foot cliff an' swims across two miles of water, just to
drop off a box of chocolates. An' y' learn from that that the
lady loves Milk Tray. And that the lady's been keepin' her legs
firmly closed. Because if she hadn't, if he'd had his way with
her he wouldn't go there by divin' off a thousand-foot cliff an'
swimmin' through a ragin' torrent. He'd go by bus. An' there'd
be no chocolates. If she mentioned the chocolates that he used
to bring he'd say, 'Oh no. I've stopped bringin' y' chocolates
babe, cos y' puttin' a bit too much weight on.' D' y' know when
y' think about it, Cadbury's could go out of business if women
didn't hold back a bit. I don't hate men. I'm not a feminist.
Not like Jane. Jane's my mate. Now she's a feminist. Well she
likes to think she is, y' know she reads Cosmopolitan an' says
that all men are potential rapists. Even the Pope. Well Jane
does hate men. She divorced her husband y' know. I never
knew him, it was before I met Jane. Apparently she came back
from work one mornin' and found her husband in bed with the
milkman. With the milkman, honest to God. Well, apparently,
from that day forward Jane was a feminist. An' I've noticed,
she never takes milk in her tea. I haven't known Jane all that
long, but she's great. She's goin' to Greece for a fortnight. Next
month she's goin'. God what will I do for two weeks? She's the
only one who keeps me sane. Jane's the only one I ever talk to,
apart from the wall – isn't she wall? She is. I said to her this
mornin', 'Jane I won't half miss y'.' You know what she said to
me? 'I want you to come with me.' (Laughs.) Silly bitch. Hey,
wall, wall, imagine the face on 'him'. Imagine the face if he
had to look after himself for two weeks. Jesus, if I go to the
bathroom for five minutes he thinks I've been hijacked.

She takes a sip of her wine.

Oh it's lovely that. It's not too dry. Some of it'd strip the palate
off y' wouldn't it. But this is lovely.

She takes another sip and savours it.

It's nice. Wine. It's like it's been kissed by the sun. 'He' doesn't drink wine. 'He' says wine is nothin' but a posh way of gettin' pissed. I suppose it is really. But it's nice. Know what I'd like to do, I'd like to drink a glass of wine in a country where the grape is grown. Sittin' by the sea. Lookin' at the sun. But 'he' won't go abroad. Well y' see, he gets jet lag when we go to the Isle of Man. An' I wouldn't mind – we go by boat. We've been goin' there for fifteen years – he still won't drink the tap water. He's that type Joe. Gets culture shock if we go to Chester. See what Jane says is, he's entitled to his own mind an' that's fine. If he doesn't wanna go abroad, well that's up to him. But that shouldn't stop me goin'. If I want to. An' I know Jane's right. I know. It's logical. Dead logical. But like I said to her, 'Jane, y' can't bring logic into this – we're talkin' about marriage.' Marriage is like the Middle East isn't it? There's no solution. You jiggle things around a bit, give up a bit here, take a bit there, deal with the flare-ups when they happen. But most of the time you just keep your head down, observe the curfew and hope that the ceasefire holds. (*Pause.*) Course, that was when Jane handed me the time bomb. She's only gone an' paid for me to go, hasn't she? She handed me the tickets this mornin'.

She goes to her bag and produces an air ticket from which she reads.

'Bradshaw. S. Mrs. BD. 581. 23 June. 19.00. From Man. to Cor.' Jane said she didn't want to go on her own. She'd just got the money through from the sale of their house. Well how the hell could I tell her it was impossible? I'll . . . I'll give her the tickets back tomorrow. She'll easy find someone else to go with her. I shouldn't have taken the bloody tickets off her in the first place. Well I tried to like, tried to expl . . ., to tell her it was impossible. But y' know what feminists are like. If something's impossible, that's the perfect reason for doin' it. Hey, wall, it'd be fantastic though, wouldn't it? I just lay his tea in front of him an' I turn away all dead casj an' say, 'Oh by the way Babe – I'm just poppin' off to Greece for a fortnight. Yeh. I just thought I'd mention it so's y' can put it in y' diary. You won't mind doin' y' own washin' an' cookin' for a couple of weeks will y' ? There's nothin' to it Doll. The white blob on the left of the kitchen is the washin' machine an' the brown blob on the right is the cooker. An' don't get them mixed up will y' or y' might end up with socks on toast.' Some chance eh wall? Some chance.

She returns the ticket to her bag.

Y' know if I said to him . . . if I said I was off to Greece for a fortnight, he'd think it was for the sex. Wouldn't he wall? Well . . . two women, on their own, goin' to Greece. Well it's obvious isn't it? I wouldn't mind – I'm not even particularly fond of it – sex, am I wall? I'm not. I think sex is like Sainsbury's – y' know, over-rated. It's just a lot of pushin' an' shovin' an' y' still come out with very little in the end. Course it would've been different if I'd been born into the next generation, our Millandra's generation. 'Cos it's different for them isn't it? They discovered it, y' see, the clitoris. 'The Clitoris Kids' I call them. And good luck to them, I don't begrudge them anythin'. But when I was a girl we'd never heard of this clitoris. In those days everyone thought it was just a case of in out, in out, shake it all about, stars'd light up the sky an' the earth would tremble. The only thing that trembled for me was the headboard on the bed. But y' see, the clitoris hadn't been discovered then, had it? I mean, obviously, it was always there, like penicillin, an' America. It was there but it's not really there until it's been discovered, is it? Maybe I should have married Christopher Columbus! I was about, about twenty-eight when I first read all about it, the clitoris. It was dead interestin'. Apparently it was all Freud's fault. Y' know, Sigmund. You see, what happened was, Freud had said that there were two ways for a woman to have erm an orgasm. An' erm the main one could only be caused by havin' the muscles, inside, stimulated. An' the other erm orgasm, it was supposed to be like an inferior, second rate one, was caused by the little clitoris. Now y' see, that's what Freud had said. An' everyone had believed him. Well, you would wouldn't y'. I mean, Sigmund Freud, who's gonna argue with Sigmund Freud. I mean, say you're just, just standin' at the bus stop, you an' Sigmund Freud, the bus comes along y' say to him, 'Does this bus go to Fazakerley,' he nods an says to y', 'Yes, this is one of the buses that goes to Fazakerley.' Well you'd get on the bus wouldn't y'? But I'll tell y' what – you'd be bloody lucky if y' ever reached Fazakerley. 'Cos Freud, y' see, he gave out the wrong information. There's only one bus that goes to Fazakerley. The clitoris bus. The other bus doesn't go anywhere near Fazakerley. But y' see everyone believed him an' they've been givin' out wrong information for years, y' know like they did with spinach. It's marvellous isn't it – tellin' people there's two kinds of orgasm. It's like tellin' people there's two Mount Everests – some people stumble onto the real mountain while the rest of us are all runnin' up this little hillock an' wonderin' why the view's not very good when we get to the top. Well when I first read about all this I was fascinated, wasn't I wall? But y' know when you read a word for the first time an' you've never heard it spoken, you can get it wrong can't y'? Y' know pronounce it wrong. Like, when I was little there was a kid in our street called Gooey. Honest. Gooey. His mother used to go 'Gooey. Y' tea's ready Gooey. Come on in Gooey.' Well y' see when she'd been lookin' for a name for him she'd been readin' this American magazine an' she saw this name, G.U.Y. Guy. But she thought it was pronounced Gooey. So that's what she christened him. Gooey McFadden he was called. Well I was the same with the clitoris. When I first read the word I thought it was pronounced clit*oris*. I still think it sounds nicer that way actually. Clit*oris*. That even sounds like it could be a name doesn't it? Clit*oris*. 'Oh hia Clit*oris*, how are y' ? Oh, really. Listen Clit*oris*, wait till I tell y' . . .'

She thinks about it.

Oh shut up wall, I think it sounds nice. Why not? There's plenty of men walkin' around called 'Dick'. Well, anyway, that's how I thought it was pronounced when I first mentioned it to Joe. We were sittin' in the front room an' I said, 'Joey. Joe have you ever heard about the clit*oris*?' He didn't even look up from his paper. 'Yeh, he said, but it doesn't go as well as the Ford Cortina.' (*Pause.*) Wait till he finds he's gettin' chips an' egg for his tea tonight. Well it's Thursday isn't it? And on Thursday it has to be mince. It's the eleventh commandment isn't it? Moses declared it. 'Thou shalt give thy feller mince every Thursday and if thou doesn't, thy feller will have one big

gob on him all night long.' What will he be like wall? What will
he be like when he sees it's only chips an' egg? An' I wouldn't
mind, it's not even my bloody fault about the mince. Well I
gave it the dog y' see. This dog at the place I work. Well it's a
bloodhound y' see. But this couple I work for – they are vegans,
y' know the vegetarian lunatic fringe – 'The Marmite Tendency'
I call them. Well they've brought up this bloodhound as a
vegetarian. Well it's not natural is it? I mean if God had
wanted to create it as a vegetarian dog he wouldn't have
created it as a bloodhound would he? He would have made it as
a grapejuice hound. But this dog is a bloodhound. It needs
meat. Well it was just on impulse really. I'm there today, an' I
looked at this dog an' all's I could think about was the pound
an' a half of best mince that's in me bag. Well d' y' know, I
think it was worth what I'll have to put up with from 'him'
tonight; just to see the look on that dog's face as it tasted meat
for the first time. Course I don't think Joe'll quite see it that
way. 'Y' did what? What did y' do? Y' gave it to the dog?
You've gone bloody mental woman. Is this it? Have y' finally
gone right round the pipe?' (*She adopts a rather grand gesture and
voice.*) 'Yes Joseph I rather think I have. I have finally gone
loop the facking loop. I have become crazy with joy, because
today Jane gave me the opportunity of getting away for a
fortnight. Joe! I am to travel to Greece with my companion.
Our departure is less than three weeks hence and we shall be
vacationing for some fourteen days. And now I must away,
leaving you to savour your chips and your chuckie egg whilst I
supervise the packing of my trunk.' (*She drops it.*) Our Brian
was round before. I showed him the tickets. Didn't I wall? An'
what did he say? 'Mother, just go. Forget about me Father,
forget about everythin', just get yourself on the plane an' go.'
(*Laughs.*) Well that's how he is, our Brian; you wanna do
somethin'? You just do it. Bugger the consequences. He's a
nutcase. But he couldn't care less. An' he's always been the
same. He was like that when he was a little kid, when he was
at school. Hey, wall, remember the Nativity play? Oh God. Our
Brian was only about eight or nine an' the school had given up
with him. The teachers just said he was loop the loop an' that
was that. I agreed with them. But the headmaster, the

headmaster was fascinated by our Brian. He like, like studied him. He said to me, there's no malice in the child, no malice whatsoever but it would appear that Brian has no concept of consequences. I think what we have to do with Brian is to try and give him more responsibility and so I've decided to give him the star part in the nativity play this year. Well when Brian learned he'd got the part of Joseph he was made up with himself. Agh, God love him, he thought he'd been picked 'cos he was great at actin' an' I couldn't say anythin' because it was workin', y' see, this psychology. All the time he's rehearsin' this nativity play his behaviour is fantastic; the headmaster's made up with him. I'm made up with him, the teachers are made up with him. An' he's made up with himself. He's practisin' every night in his room – (*One note.*) 'We are weary travellers on our way to Bethlehem an' my wife is having a baby an' we need to rest at the Inn for the night.' Well the day of the show, I got down to the school, the play started an' it was lovely, y' know all the little angels came on an' they all have a sly little wave to their Mams. Then it was our Brian's entrance; he comes on an' he's pullin' this donkey behind him – it's like this hobby horse on wheels. An' perched on top of it is this little girl, takin' the part of the Virgin Mary an' she's dressed beautiful, y' know her Mother's really dolled her up to be the part. An' she's givin' a little wave to her Mam. So Brian gives the donkey a bit of a tug because he's takin' it dead serious an' he doesn't believe they should be wavin' to their Mams. He's up there, he's actin' like he might win The Oscar – y' know he's mimin' givin' hay to the donkey an' he's pattin' it on the head. Well the headmaster turned round an' smiled at me. I think he was as proud of our Brian as I was. Well Brian gets to the door of the Inn and he goes knock knock knock an' the little Inkeeper appears. Our Brian starts 'We are weary travellers on our way to Bethlehem an' my wife is havin' a baby an' we need to rest for the night at the Inn.' So the little feller playin' the Innkeeper pipes up, 'You cannot stay at the Inn because the Inn is full up an' there is no room at the Inn.' An' then our Brian is supposed to say somethin' like: 'Well we must go an' find a lowly cattle shed an' stay in there.' Then he's supposed to go off pullin' the donkey, an' the Virgin Mary behind him. But he didn't. Well, I don't

know if it's the Virgin Mary, gettin' up our Brian's nose,
because she's spent the whole scene wavin' to her Mother or
whether it was just that our Brian suddenly realised that the
part of Joseph wasn't as big as it had been cracked up to be.
But whatever it was, instead of goin' off pullin' the donkey, he
suddenly turned to the little Inkeeper an' yelled at him – 'Full
up? Full up? But we booked!' Well the poor little Inkeeper
didn't know what day of the week it was. He's lookin' all round
the hall for someone to rescue him an' his bottom lip's beginnin'
to tremble an' our Brian's goin' – 'Full up? I've got the wife
outside, waitin' with the donkey. She's expectin' a baby any
minute now, there's snow everywhere in six foot drifts an' you're
trying' to tell me that you're full up?' Well the top brass on the
front row are beginnin' to look a bit uncomfortable – they're
beginnin' to turn an' look at the headmaster an' our Brian's
givin' a perfect imitation of his father, on a bad day; he's
beratin' anythin' that dares move. The little Innkeeper's lip is
goin' ten to the dozen an' the Virgin Mary's in floods of tears on
the donkey. Well the Innkeeper finally grasps that the script is
well out of the window an' that he has to do somethin' about
our Brian. So he steps forward an' he says, 'Listen Mate, listen!
I was only jokin'. We have got room really. Y' can come in if y'
want.' An' with that the three of them disappeared into the Inn.
End of Nativity play an' the end of our Brian's actin' career.
Me an' our Brian, we sometimes have a laugh about it now, but
at the time I could have died of shame. It was all over the
papers: 'Mary and Joseph Fail To Arrive In Bethlehem.' I was
ashamed. (*Pause.*) It's no wonder really, that I've never
travelled anywhere meself; it must be God punishin' me for
raisin' a child who managed to prevent Mary an' Joseph
reachin' their destination. An' there was me when I was a girl –
the only thing I ever wanted to do was travel. I always wanted
to be a, a courier. Or an air hostess. But it was only the clever
ones who got to do things like that. When I got my final report
from school, the headmistress had written at the bottom of it, 'I
can confidently predict that Miss Valentine . . .', that was me
maiden name, 'I confidently predict that Miss Valentine will not
go far in life. I feel this is just as well for, given her marks in
geography, she would surely get lost.' She was a mare that

headmistress. She used to come into assembly sometimes an'
ask like a spot question, an' whoever got it right would get
loads of housepoints, an' it was nearly always Marjorie Majors
who got it right – she took private elocution lessons an' she left
school with just under four billion housepoints. One day, we
were all standin' there in assembly an' this headmistress
appeared; 'A question,' she said to everyone, 'a question: what
was man's most important invention?' Well every hand in the
hall shot up. 'Me Miss,' 'I know Miss,' 'Miss, Miss, me Miss.'
An' my hand was up with the rest of them because for once I
knew the answer. But this headmistress, she took one look at
me an' said, 'Oh put your hand down Shirley, you won't know
the answer,' an' she started goin' round the hall, the grin on her
face gettin' smugger an' smugger as she got answers like, 'the
sputnik', 'the cathode ray tube,' 'the automatic washin'
machine.' Even the clever ones were gettin' it wrong – even
Marjorie Majors. But I kept my arm up there in the air because
I knew I had the right answer. I'd got it from me Dad an' he'd
got it from the Encyclopaedia Britannica. Agh, y' know me
Dad, he was still goin' on about that Encyclopaedia Britannica
when he was on his death bed. 'How can those kids of mine be
so thick when I bought them the Encyclopaedia Britannica?' He
got a lot of pleasure out of it though. He'd sit there for hours
readin' it an' then he'd try to impress us all with these dead odd
facts. An' I'd remembered him sayin' about man's most
important invention because it was so ordinary. So I'm stood
there in assembly, me arm stuck up in the air, an' I am like the
cat with the cream because this headmistress has done the
length an' breadth of the hall an' still no-one's come up with the
right answer. Well I'm the only one left so she turns to me an'
she says, 'All right then Shirley, come on, you might as well get
it wrong along with everyone else. Do you remember the
question Shirley – what was man's most important invention?'
Well I paused, y' know savourin' the moment, knowin' I was on
the brink of receivin' at least forty three thousand housepoints
an' a blessin' from the Pope. But when I said, 'the wheel', it
was like this headmistress had been shot in the back. I thought
maybe she hadn't heard me squeaky little voice so I said it
again, louder, 'The wheel Miss, man's most important invention

was . . .' But I never got to finish because I was cut off by this scream from the headmistress. 'YOU,' she yelled, 'You must have been told that answer!' I just stood there, reelin' with shock. An' I tried to ask her, to say, to say, how . . . how the bloody hell else I was supposed to learn the right answer. But she wouldn't listen. She just ignored me an' told the demented music teacher to get on with playin' the hymn. An' all me housepoints, an' me blessin' from the Pope just disappeared before me eyes as she led the hall into singin' 'Glad That I Live Am I.' I was never really interested in school after that. I became a rebel. I wore me school skirt so high y' would've thought it was a serviette. I was marvellous. I used to have the chewy goin' all day, like that (*Chewing.*) an' I'd just exude boredom out of every pore. I hated everythin'. 'Oh I hate him', 'Oh I hate her,' 'I hate this, I hate that.' 'It's garbage,' 'It's last,' 'It's crap.' 'I hate it.' But I didn't hate anythin' y' know. The only thing I hated was me. I didn't want to be a rebel. I wanted to be nice. I wanted to be like Marjorie Majors. I used to pick on her somethin' rotten an' I really wanted to be like her. Can't y' be evil when you're a kid? I saw her a few weeks ago, Marjorie Majors. Didn't I wall? I hadn' even heard of her for years. I'm in town, loaded down with shoppin' an' what's the first thing that always happens when y' in town loaded down with shoppin'? Right. The heavens opened. An' it's funny the way all these things are linked but they are; once you're in town, loaded with shoppin' bags, caught in a deluge – it always follows that every bus ever made disappears off the face of the earth. Well I'm standin' there, like a drowned rat, me hair's in ruins an' I've got mascara lines runnin' from me face to me feet, so I thought I might as well trudge up to the Adelphi an' get a taxi. Course when I got there the taxis had gone into hidin' along with the buses. Well I'm just rootin' in me bag, lookin' for somethin' to slash me wrists with when this big white car pulls up to the hotel an' of course I'm standin' right by a puddle an' as the wheels go through it, half the puddle ends up over me an' the other half in me shoppin' bags. Well all I wanted to do by this time was scream. So I did. I just opened me mouth, standin' there in front of the hotel an' let out this scream. I could've been arrested but I didn't care. Well I was in mid-scream when I noticed this woman get out the white car an' start comin' towards me. An' she's dead elegant. Y' know she's walkin' through this torrential rain an' I guarantee not one drop of it was landin' on her. But the second she opened her mouth I knew who she was. I'd recognise those elocution lessons anywhere. 'Forgive me for asking,' she said, 'but didn't you used to be Shirley Valentine?' I just stood there, starin'. And drippin'. 'It is,' she said, 'it's Shirley,' an' the next thing, she's apologisin' for half drownin' me an' she's pullin' me into the hotel an' across the lobby an' into this lounge that's the size of two football pitches. Well, she's ordered tea an' I'm sittin' there, rain water drippin' down me neck an' plastic carrier bags round me feet an' I'm thinkin', 'Well Marjorie, you've waited a long time for your revenge but you've got me good style now, haven't y'? Well go on, spare me the torture, just put the knife in quick an' let's get it over with; come on tell me all about your bein' an air hostess on Concorde.' But she didn't say anythin'. She just sat there, lookin' at me, y' know really lookin' at me. I thought I'm not gonna let her milk it so I said, 'You're an' air hostess these days are y' Marjorie? Oh yes, I hear it's marvellous. You travel all over the world don't you?' But she still just kept lookin' at me. The waitress was just puttin' the tea an' cakes on the table in front of us. I said to her 'This is my friend Marjorie. We were at school together. Marjorie's an air hostess.' 'An air hostess?' Marjorie suddenly said, 'Darling whatever gave you that idea? I certainly travel widely but I'm not an air hostess. Shirley, I'm a hooker. A whore.' Marjorie Majors – a high class hooker! 'Oh really Marjorie,' I said, 'An' all that money your mother spent on elocution lessons.' By this time, the waitress was pourin' the tea into the cream buns! Well me an' Marjorie – God, we had a great afternoon together. She didn't come lordin' it over me at all. Y' know she told me about all the places she works – Bahrain, New York, Munich. An' d' y' know what she told me? When we were at school . . . She wanted to be like me. The two of us, sittin' there at the Adelphi, one's like somethin' out of Dynasty, one's like somethin' out of the bagwash an' we're havin' a great time confessin' that all those years ago, we each wanted to be the other. I was sad when I thought about it. Like

the two of us could have been great mates – y' know real close.
We didn't half get on well together, that afternoon, in the
Adelphi. We were rememberin' all kinds. I could've sat there
forever – neither of us wanted to leave. But then the time
caught up with us an' Marjorie had to get her plane. An' y'
know somethin' – she didn't want to go. Paris she had to go to,
Paris France, an' she didn't want to. An' an' on the way out
. . . d' y' know what she did? She leaned forward an' just
kissed me – there on the cheek – an' there was real affection in
that kiss. It was the sweetest kiss I'd known in years. An' then
she, she held my shoulders an' looked at me and said, 'Goodbye
Shirley. Goodbye, Shirley Valentine.' (*Pause.*) On the way
home, on the bus, I was cryin'. I don't know why. I'm starin'
out the window, tears trippin' down me cheeks. An' in me head
there's this voice that keeps sayin', 'I used to be Shirley
Valentine. I used to be Shirley Valentine . . . I used to be
Shirley . . .' (*She is crying.*) What happened? Who turned me
into this? I don't want this. Do you remember her wall?
Remember Shirley Valentine? She got married to a boy called
Joe an' one day she came to live here. An' an' even though her
name was changed to Bradshaw she was still Shirley Valentine.
For a while. She still . . . knew who she was. She used to . . .
laugh. A lot. Didn't she? She used to laugh with Joe – when the
pair of them did things together, when they made this kitchen
together an' painted it together. Remember wall? Remember
when they first painted you an' an' the silly buggers painted
each other as well. Stood here, the pair of them, havin' a paint
fight, coverin' each other from head to foot in yellow paint. An'
then the two of them, thinkin' they're dead darin', gettin' in the
bath – together. And the water was so yellow that he said it
was like gettin' a bath in vanilla ice cream. And Shirley
Valentine washed his hair . . . and kissed his wet head . . . and
knew what happiness meant. What happened wall? What
happened to the pair of them – to Joe, to Shirley Valentine. Did
somethin' happen or was it just that nothin' happened? It would
be . . . easier to understand if somethin' had happened, if I'd
found him in bed with the milkman, if, if there was somethin'
to blame. But there's nothin'. They got married, they made a
home, they had kids and brought them up. And somewhere

along the way the boy called Joe turned into 'him' and Shirley
Valentine turned into this and what I can't remember is the day
or the week or the month or the . . . when it happened. When it
stopped bein' good. When Shirley Valentine disappeared,
became just another name on the missin' persons list.

She makes a partially successful attempt to change gear.

He says he still loves me y' know. But he doesn't. It's just
somethin' he says. It's terrible – 'I love you,' isn't it? Like, like
it's supposed to make everythin' all right. You can be beaten
an' battered an' half insane an' if you complain he'll say, he'll
say, 'what's wrong, y' know I love you.' 'I Love You'. They
should bottle it an' sell it. It cures everythin'. And d' y' know
somethin'? I've always wondered . . . why . . . is it that if
somebody says – I love you it seems to automatically give them
the right . . . to treat you worse . . . than people they only like,
or people they don't like at all, or people they couldn't care less
about. See, see, if I wasn't my feller's . . . wife. If I was just a
next door neighbour or the man in the paper shop – he'd talk to
me nice. An' he doesn't say he loves the next door neighbour or
the feller in the paper shop – he says he loves me! An' he
doesn't talk nice to me. When he talks to me at all. It's funny
isn't it – 'I love you.'

Pause as she begins the final stage in the cooking of the meal.

An' I know what you're sayin'. You're sayin' what Jane always
says – why don't I leave? An' the fact of the matter is – I don't
know why. I don't know why anyone should put up with a
situation in which a forty-two-year-old woman has the
opportunity of fulfillin' a dream, of travellin', just a little bit,
just two weeks of the year, an' can't do it. I don't know why
. . . I just know that if y' described me to me, I'd say you were
tellin' me a joke. I don't know why I stay. I hate it. I hate the
joke of it. I hate a life of talkin' to the wall. But I've been
talkin' to the wall for more years than I care to remember now.
An' I'm frightened. I'm frightened of life beyond the wall. When
I was a girl I used to jump off our roof. For fun. Now I get
vertigo just standin' on the pavement. I'm terrified if y' want to
know. I'm terrified that if I left him, I'd have nowhere to go,

an' I'd find that there was no place for me in the life beyond
the wall – they'd kept a place reserved for me. For a while. But
when it seemed I wasn't comin' back they gave the place to
someone else – maybe someone younger, someone who could
still talk the language of the place beyond the wall. So I stay.
Here. An' . . . an' if I have to give up goin' to Greece – well
. . . sod it. I mean, after all, what's the Acropolis? It's only an
old fashioned ruin, isn't it? It's like the DJ's say, isn't it? 'We're
all scousers – there's nothin' wrong with us – we've always got a
laugh an' a joke haven't we? They're not like us in London are
they? Not like us in Greece are they? Greece? Y' know what
Greece is, don't y' love? Greece is what y' cook his egg an' chips
in. (*Laughs.*) (*Pause.*) An' anyway, another bottle of Riesling I'll
be able to pretend this is Greece. Hey, wall . . . look. (*Goes to
the window.*) Look at the sun an' the way it's shinin'. Look at
the sea, the sea. Smell the honeysuckle. Can't you just taste
those olives, those grapes. Look wall, look at that woman, that
lovely woman – doesn't she look serene, sittin' beneath a
parasol, at a table by the sea, drinking wine in a country where
the grape is grown.

As she lays a plate on the table, the backdoor opens.

Blackout.

Scene Two

Three weeks later/the kitchen.

*A suitcase stands in the kitchen. SHIRLEY enters. She is dressed in a
fairly formal and attractive two-piece suit, wears high heels and carries
a hat which she places on top of the suitcase, and a large leather
handbag/shoulder bag which she places on top of one of the work
surfaces. Throughout the scene she constantly double and even triple
checks details of the kitchen, contents of cupboards, whereabouts of
utensils. When first she enters she is in a state of nervous agitation.*

SHIRLEY. Guess where I'm goin'? Jane's booked a taxi to take
us to the airport. She's pickin' me up at four o'clock.
(*Suddenly.*) Four o'clock. (*Checking clock and her watch.*) Oh Jeez
oh Jeez. Passport. Passport. (*Checks the contents of her handbag.*)

Passport, tickets, money. Passport, tickets, money. Yeh. Oh
God, oh God please say it will be all right. O I feel sick. Those
travel sickness pills mustn't be workin' – I still feel sick an' I've
taken four already. An' I've only travelled up an' down the
stairs. Oh God, passport, tickets, money, passport. I got a full
one, a proper passport. Well you never know Shirley – it could
be the start of somethin' – this year Greece, next year . . . the
world.

Slaps the passport shut with a cry of strained anguish.

Ogh. I know I should have told him. I know it would have been
easier if I'd told him. It wouldn't though, would it wall. If I'd
told him he would have talked me out of it. He would have
found a way. He would have made me feel guilty. Guilty? As if
I don't feel guilty enough as it is. Three weeks, secretly gettin'
all me things ready. It's been like livin' in bleedin' Colditz with
a tunnel beneath the floorboards an' every soddin' sound y'
think it's the SS, comin' for y' – they've found out about the
tunnel. (*She looks up.*) God. God I know . . . I'm bein' cruel. I
know I'll have to pay for it, when I get back. But I don't mind
payin' for it then. Just . . . just do me a big favour God an'
don't make me have to pay for it durin' this fortnight. Don't let
anythin' happen to our Millandra, our Brian. An' keep Joe
safe. Please. (*Pause.*) Three weeks secretly ironin' an' packin'
an' cookin' all his meals for this two weeks. They're all in the
freezer. Me Mother's gonna come in an' defrost them an' do his
cookin'. With a bit of luck 'he' won't even notice I'm not here.
Oh I'll have to leave him a note. 'Gone to Greece – Back in two
weeks.' Ogh, you should've told him. Y' should have Shirley.
Shirley, y' silly bitch. How could you have told him an' still
been able to go? I know, I know. An' look what happened over
the chips and egg. I know I know. (*Pause.*) Keep thinkin' about
the chips an' egg, keep thinkin' about the . . . It was that that
decided me, wasn't it wall? I'd cooked those chips lovely, hadn't
I? In oil. An' they were free range those eggs. I mean, all right,
so he was expectin' mince but . . . he sits down at that table,
doesn't he, an' he looks at this plate of egg an' chips. Just
looks. Doesn't make any effort to pick up his knife an' fork. He
sits there, with this dead quizzical look on his face, an' he's

starin' at the plate, studyin' it, y' know as though it contains
the meanin' of life. Well I just ignored him didn't I? I just sat
there, at the other end of the table. Well, eventually, he goes,
'What's this? What. Is. This?' I said to him, I said, 'Well when
I cooked it, it was egg an' chips, an' as neither of us is Paul
Daniels I'm assumin' it still is egg an' chips.' Well he leaned
back in his chair an' he said, 'I am not . . . eating shit,' honest
to God, an' he pushed the plate the entire length of the table.
Well I'm sittin' there then, aren't I? With a lap full of egg an'
chips. I've got yolk, drippin' down me leg an' 'he' has started
talkin' to the fridge; 'cos he does that, when he's narked,
doesn't he wall. If he's in a real nark he always talks to the
cooker or the fridge or the mantelpiece. 'I'm pullin' me tripe out
from mornin' till night,' he's tellin' the fridge, 'An' what does
she give me when I get home.' Well of course, the fridge never
answers him so whenever he asks it a question, he always
answers it himself. He always goes – 'I'll tell y' what she gives
me. Chips an' egg, chips an' fuckin' egg she gives me.' Well I
don't know what possessed me but while he was screamin' at
the fridge, I picked meself up from the table, cleaned meself
down as best I could, got hold of a pen an' wrote, across the
wall, in big letters – GREECE. He didn't even notice, 'cos by
this time he's givin' the cooker an' the fridge his impression of
Ian Paisley deliverin' the Gettysburg Address. Well I just
walked out. I got me coat an' went round to our Millandra's
flat. But there was no-one in. I just walked round the block a
few times. I was gonna phone Jane but all the phones were out
of order. They always are aren't they? Well they are round here
– even the vandals are complainin'. I must have walked round
for about an hour. I wanted to go an' see someone, someone I
could talk to. But there wasn't anyone. I never felt so alone in
me whole life. I used to know so many people. Where does
everyone go to? In the end I just came back here. He'd been to
a Chinese take-away. 'What's that?' he said to me, pointin' at
the wall. 'It's a place,' I said. 'It's a place I'm goin' to.' 'I'm not
goin' to no Greece,' he said. 'If that's why I'm not gettin' fed
properly, because you're savin' up for a foreign holiday, y' can
forget it.' Well that's when I started laughin'. I ended up . . . I
was hysterical . . . I ended up rollin' on the kitchen floor. He

just stepped over me, walked out. But I couldn't stop laughin'
because I knew then. I knew I was gonna do it. I knew I was
gonna go to Greece. An' everythin' went marvellous didn't it? I
made all the arrangements, got me passport. I was quite
impressed with meself. So yesterday I thought I'd nip into town
an' get a few last minute things, know the way y' do? Well as I
passed Marks an' Spencers I looked in the window an' y' know
they had some lovely underwear on display, y' dead silky. A
little bit Janet Reger but only half the price. Well normally I'm
a bit conservative – next to the skin as it were – but I thought
oh go on, give y'self a treat, it's the sort of stuff that'd be nice
and cool in a hot climate. So I get into Marks, I bought a new
bra, a couple of slips, a few pairs of pants an' I'm standin'
there waitin' for them to be wrapped. Well who comes up to me
but 'her' from next door. Gillian. Well what's she like wall?
What's Gillian like? I'm not sayin' she's a bragger, but if you've
been to Paradise, she's got a season ticket. Y' know she's that
type – if you've got a headache, she's got a brain tumour. 'Oh
hello Shirley,' she says, 'cos that's how she talks, know she
begrudges y' the breath. 'Hello Shirley, oh they're nice,' she
said, spottin' me little garments. 'It's marvellous what they can
do with man-made fibres these days isn't it?' An' she's pickin'
up one of me slips y' know, havin' a really good gawp at it.
'You'd almost think it was silk. If you weren't familiar with the
real thing.' I said to meself, 'Keep your mouth shut Shirley.'
Because y' can't win with her. Well she dropped the slip back
on the counter an' then she said, 'But I suppose they will look
quite nice on your Millandra.' Well I know I should've kep me
mouth shut but that got me really riled an' I suddenly heard
meself sayin', 'Oh no Gillian these aren't for Millandra, I'm
buyin' these for meself. Of course, I shan't be wearin' them for
meself, I shall be wearin' them for me lover.' Well her jaw
dropped into her handbag. For once she couldn't top it an' I got
a bit carried away then. I heard meself sayin', 'Yes Gillian, we
fly out tomorrow, my lover and I, for a fortnight in the Greek
Islands – just two weeks of sun, sand, taramasalata an'
whatever else takes our fancy. Well I must be goin' Gillian –
I've still got a few things to buy. I don't suppose you've noticed
which counter the suspender belts are on? Oh well never mind,

I'll find them. Tarar Gillian,' an' I was off before she could get
her wits together an' tell me about the two-year fling she's been
havin' with Robert Redford. Course, all the way home on the
bus I'm thinkin', 'Oh you silly bitch. Why did you say that?
What happens if she calls round tonight – while 'he's' in? What
happens if she just lets it slip?' 'Cos she's like that Gillian, y'
know she's got more news than Channel Four. But when I got
home I forgot all about Gillian. When I got home, what was
waitin' for me? Our Millandra, with all her bags an' cases. 'I
hate that Sharron-Louise,' she said. 'She's a mare. Mother, I've
come back to live with you.' Well I'm stood here lookin' at her,
me jaw's dropped halfway to Australia. 'Mother,' she says,
'Will y' make me some Horlicks an' toast – like y' used to?'
Then she was off. Up the stairs to her old room. Well I made
her the toast an' the Horlicks – took it up to her. She's got
herself into bed, sittin' there propped up with two pillows,
readin' her old Beano annuals. 'I love you Mother,' she said, 'I
don't know why I went to live with that cow in the first place,
Mother y' haven't put enough sugar in this Horlicks will y' get
us another spoon?' Well I go down, get the sugar, bring it back,
stir it up for her an' she's sayin' 'We'll go down town on
Saturday shall we Mother? We'll do a bit of shoppin' eh
Mother, just you an' me.' An' the thing is, I was noddin'. She
hadn't been back ten minutes an' I'd gone straight into bein'
'Auto-Mother'. She's got me struttin' round like R2 bleedin' D2.
Well it was when she asked me to bring the telly upstairs for
her that me head cleared. Instead of goin' downstairs again I
sat on the edge of the bed an' I said, 'Millandra, I'm really
pleased you've come back home because I've missed y'. I mean,
I've never said that or whinged an' whined because I believe
that kids have to have their own lives. But there's many a time
y' know, many a time that I would have loved to sit down with
y' an' talk, go to town with y', have a meal with y', share a
laugh, just, like not as your mother but as another human
bein'. But I couldn't because you had your own life, your own
friends, your own interests – none of it to do with me.' 'Well
we'll be able to do all that now,' she said, 'because I've come
back home.' 'And that's fantastic,' I said. 'An' you couldn't
have picked a better time – it'll be a great help havin' you here

to look after your father.' Well this look came on her face,
'What's wrong with him?' she said. 'Oh there's nothin' wrong
with him,' I assured her, 'But y' know with me not bein' here,
with me an' Jane goin' to Greece tomorrow.' Well, d' y' know,
it was like her hot water bottle had sprung a leak. 'What?' she
yelled. 'Yeh,' I said, 'I'm goin' to Greece for a fortnight.' 'You,'
she said, 'You, goin' to Greece, what for?' 'For two weeks,' I said.
Well she flounces out of the bed, 'That Jane one, an' you,' she's
goin', 'In Greece. An' what's me Father had to say about that?'
Well when I said I hadn't told him, she went mental. She
started gettin' dressed, 'I think it's a disgrace,' she's goin', 'Two
middle aged women goin' on their own to Greece – I think it's
disgustin'.' An' she's straight down the stairs an' on the phone,
tellin' Sharron-Louise that she's comin' back to the flat. Well
I'm sittin' there upstairs an' then it suddenly struck me – her
sayin' I was disgustin'. I mean she's jumpin' to the same
conclusions as her Father would. She thinks I'm just goin' off
on a grab a granny fortnight. Well I started to get narked then.
The more I thought about it, the more riled I got. I was gonna
go down an' give her a piece of me mind but I heard the front
door slam. I went to the window an' she's loadin' her things
into a taxi. Well I flung the window open an' I shouted, 'Yes,
that's right Millandra – I'm goin' to Greece for the sex; sex for
breakfast, sex for dinner, sex for tea an' sex for supper.' Well
she just ignored me but this little cab driver leans out an' pipes
up, 'That sounds like a marvellous diet love.' 'It is,' I shouted
down, 'Have y' never heard of it? It's called the 'F' Plan.' Well
our Millandra slammed the taxi door an' off they went down
the street. I just sat there in our Millandra's bedroom. I was
livid at first but when I calmed down I just felt . . . felt like a
real fool. All I could think about was Millandra sayin' 'What
for. You goin' to Greece – what for?' Kids – they can't half
destroy your confidence can't they? I'd spent three weeks tellin'
meself I could do it, that I'd be all right, be able to go, be able
to enjoy meself. I'd even convinced meself that I wasn't really
that old, that me hips weren't really as big as I thought they
were, that me belly was quite flat for a woman who's had two
kids. That me stretch marks wouldn't really be noticeable to
anyone but me. I'd even let that salesgirl at C&A sell me a

bikini. But sittin' there on our Millandra's bed, after she'd said
that – I suddenly had thighs that were thicker than the pillars
in the Parthenon. Me stretch marks were as big as tyre marks
on the M6 an' instead of goin' to Greece I should be applyin' for
membership of the pensioners' club. I'm sittin' there thinkin',
maybe our Millandra's right. 'You goin' to Greece. What for?'
Maybe she's right, maybe it is pathetic. What am I goin' for? I
mean, it might be easier not to go, to stay here. Where I'm
safe. Where there's no risk. For three weeks I'd been buildin' up
this marvellous picture of what it would be like, how I was goin'
to feel with the sun on me an' the ocean everywhere. But after
she'd said that I couldn't . . . couldn't get the picture back, into
me mind. I couldn't bring back the feelin' I'd had. I just sat
there thinkin', 'Shirley you are one silly bitch. Just another
stupid woman who thinks she can have an adventure, when the
time for adventures is over.' 'What for?' I kept askin' meself. I
thought about the bikini I'd bought an' I felt ashamed. I felt
embarrassed at me own stupidity, at lettin' meself think it was
possible. 'What for?' 'What am I goin' for?' An' of course the
truth of the matter was that I was goin' for the excitement of
not knowing; not knowing where I was goin', not knowing what
would happen, not knowing what the place would be like or
look like, not knowin' just how hot the sun would feel, not
knowin' the foreign language I'd hear, not knowin', for the first
time since before I could remember, exactly what the days
would hold for me. It was the excitement of somethin' that was
foreign, to me. The excitement of jumpin' off our roof. An'
when our Millandra had said that; it was like, like she'd caught
me, on the roof, just as I was about to jump an' she'd said,
''Ey, you'll break your bloody neck. Get down off there an'
don't be so stupid.' An' I hesitated, an' in that moment I saw
how big the drop was, an' how hard the ground was an' how
fragile me bones were. An' I realised that I was too old for
jumpin' off the roof. I went downstairs, to phone Jane, to phone
me mother an' tell her she needn't bother comin' in for the
fortnight. I'd even picked up the phone. But the doorbell went
an' I put the phone down an' went to the door. Gillian was
stood there. 'Oh hello Shirley,' she said, 'Is Joe at home?' Well I
just laughed. 'No Joe's not in Gillian. But listen, if you've come

to spill the beans, y' might as well . . .' But she just pushed past me, came into the house. 'I don't want to spill any beans, Shirley,' she said, 'I just wanted to check that Joe wasn't in before I gave you this,' an' she handed me this beautifully wrapped package. 'I want you to have this Shirley. It's never been worn. You see,' she said, 'I was never . . . brave enough. Oh Shirley,' she said, 'How I wish I had. How I wish I'd had your . . . bravery.' With that she went to the door. Just as she was goin' out she said to me – 'You're brave Shirley. I just want you to know, I think you're marvellous,' an' she was gone. I opened up the package. (*Shirley opens the case.*) It was this. (*Produces a superb silk robe.*) Silk. Gillian was right – there's nothin' like the real thing. It must have been bought years an' years ago. It's got the original label – The Bon Marche. I didn't even dare try it on at first. I felt awful, about what I'd said to Gillian, about taking a lover. I mean, I didn't think she'd really believe me. But she had. Completely believed me. Gillian believed that it was perfectly possible for me to be some marvellous, brave, living woman. I got me mirror out an' looked at meself, an' tried to see the woman that Gillian had seen in me. In Gillian's eyes I was no longer Shirley the neighbour, Shirley the middle-aged mother, Shirley Bradshaw. I had become Shirley The Sensational, Shirley The Brave, Shirley Valentine. An' even if I couldn't see it in the mirror, even if none of it was true about me takin' a lover an' all that rubbish – the point is that Gillian had believed it. Believed it was possible of me. I tried the robe on. It was perfect. It was beautiful. An' in that moment . . . so was I. In that moment our roof wouldn't have been high enough for me. I could have jumped off a skyscraper. An' now the day's here. An' I'm goin'. I'm goin' to the land beyond the wall. I'm gonna sit an' eat olives on a Greek seafront. An' I don't even like olives. But I might like them in Greece. They eat squid y' know. An' octopus – they do. An' I'm gonna eat it too. I don't care. I'm gonna do everythin'. I'm gonna try anything. Like I used to. Unafraid. Without fear of anythin' new. I'll be Shirley The Brave. Course, I'm terrified really. But I'm not gonna let it show. I'm not gonna let it stop me from enjoyin' things. I don't mean I'm gonna be a girl again – because you can never be that; but

instead of sayin' 'Christ, I'm forty-two.' I'm gonna say –
'Shirley, you're only forty-two, isn't that marvellous.' (*She looks
at herself in the mirror.*) Not bad, not bad. Oh hold on, hold on.

She places the hat on her head and examines the effect in the mirror.

What do you think wall? Oh shut up wall, I'm not talkin' to
you. (*She smiles at herself in the mirror.*) Well, that's it Shirley –
all dolled up an' ready to go. Case packed? Case packed.
Passport, tickets, money? Passport, tickets, money.

*She closes her handbag and sits with it, on the suitcase. She takes a
last glance at the kitchen to see if everything has been left in order. It
has.*

Four o'clock Jane's pickin' me up. (*She looks at her watch.*)
Twenty past two.

Blackout

ACT TWO

Scene One

A secluded section of shore, dotted with rocks and baked by the Mediterranean sun. It is an underdeveloped corner of the bay, a place not yet appropriated by tourists. In the background we can see a hint of the village and the taverna. The deep blue of the sky dominates. A white table with parasol and some chairs has been placed in this spot. When we open, the parasol is still folded. There is a piece of rush matting laid out for sun-bathing. SHIRLEY enters. She has bare feet and wears GILLIAN's robe.

SHIRLEY. I'll bet y' didn't recognise me did y'? I hardly recognise meself these days. D' y' like me tan?

She opens the robe to display a deep tan. She wears only cut down denims and a bikini top.

It's marvellous isn't it? I love it here – don't I rock? (*Points to rock.*) That's rock. We met the first day I got here, didn't we? Well I didn't want to go down onto the beach y' see. I thought I'd get a bit of a tan before I ventured onto the beach because – let's face it – I was so white. If I'd walked onto that beach when I first got here, they would have thought I'd just had a fresh coat of white emulsion. When I first arrived there was more glare comin' off me than there was off the sun. So what I did, was I found this little place – I found you, didn't I rock? I talked to you. Rock. He's got his name written all the way through him. Course, I talk to rock – but he doesn't talk back to me. Well he can't can he? It's a Greek rock. It doesn't understand a bleedin' word I'm sayin'. I might have risked the beach if I'd been with Jane. But on me own I felt a bit . . . y' know conspicuous. Jane met a feller didn't she? Not here – on the plane – honest to God. An' the state of him. I wouldn't give y' tuppence a ton. Sporty type – y' know all groin an' Adidas labels. OOOgh. Designer teeth he had. An' bloodshot eyes. Y' know when he smiled with these blazin' white teeth an' the bloodshot eyes, I said to Jane, 'Oh he must be a Liverpool supporter.' She didn't like that. But I didn't care. I'd got past carin' to tell y' the truth. I mean, we were gonna do everythin' together. We hadn't even landed an' she's got herself fixed up. She only went to the loo. When she got back she said to me, 'Erm, I've just been invited out to dinner. Tonight.' Well I looked at her, 'Pardon,' I said. 'Yeh,' she said, 'I've just met this chap, sittin' up at the back. He's stayin' at a villa on the other side of the Island an' he's invited me over for dinner. Tonight. Oh Shirley you don't mind do you?' Well I didn't say anythin'. There was nothin' I could say was there? I just stared out the window of the plane an' I thought, 'D' y' know, if I had a parachute, I'd get off now.' I even considered gettin' off without a parachute actually. Course she was sayin' to me – 'It's only for tonight. We'll still do all the things we planned Shirley.' But I knew. Me instinct told me I'd hardly see her again after that. An' I didn't want her to be spendin' time with me when she'd rather be elsewhere. I didn't want her pityin' me. 'Listen Jane,' I said, 'I think you've probably blown the feminist of the year award – so will y' just leave it out, right? Obviously,' I said, 'It's been a difficult time for you since your feller ran off with the milkman and now that you've got this opportunity I don't want y' to give even a thought of me. You just go off to his villa an' enjoy yourself an' give his olives a good pressing.' D' y' know what she said to me? 'Thanks for bein' so understandin'.' An' she never came back that night y' know. Or the next mornin'. She never came back for the first four days. They must've been marvellous olives. I was just left on me own. I was alone. But I wasn't lonely. Well I'm an expert at it really. But what I found was – if you're a woman, alone, it doesn't half seem to upset people; like whenever I walked into the dinin' room at the hotel it was like everyone was lookin' at me. I've got this little table to meself, an' it's lovely. I just love sittin' there, in the evenin'. But on the third day, I'm sat there at me table. I've been sunbathin' all day, I'm glowin' like a lobster an' feelin' dead content an' quiet. I was in such a trance I hadn't even noticed this woman come across. She was talkin' to me before I realised she was there. 'We couldn't help notice you were alone dear,' she says to me,

'Would y' like to come an' join us at our table? There is a spare place.' Well I was shattered. I didn't want to join anyone. I didn't wanna talk. I wanted to be quiet. But she's standin' there, waitin' for me to say somethin'. An' then I notice that the whole of the restaurant's waitin' as well. All of them lookin', waitin' to see what would happen to the woman on her own. Well, of course, I couldn't say no, could I? I mean the woman was only bein' kind wasn't she? But inside I was cursin'. Well d' y' know, as I sat down at their table, with her an' her husband, it was like the whole of the restaurant let out this great sigh of relief, as if me bein' on me own had been like a great problem for everyone, an' now it had been solved, everyone could relax, everyone could talk louder an' laugh; I thought the waiters were gonna break into applause 'cos I'd been rescued from me loneliness by Jeanette an' Dougie. Jeanette an' Dougie Walsh – from Manchester. Well, I know the exact dimensions of her kitchen, the price of the new extension, the colour of the microwave an' the contents of the Hoover, an' we hadn't even started on the first course; it's a good job it wasn't soup – I would've put me head in it an' drowned meself. It wasn't until we got to the main course that they even acknowledged we were in Greece. And then I wish they hadn't bothered. Everything was wrong – the sun was too hot for them, the sea was too wet for them, Greece too Greek for them. They were that type, y' know, if they'd been at the last supper they would have asked for chips. An' I wouldn't mind but the family on the next table joined in as well an' started complainin' about everythin'. An' I'm sittin' there dead embarrassed out of me mind because there's this poor Greek waiter tryin' to serve our main course an' he's got to listen to this lot goin' about his country as though it's in the Fourth World. This feller on the table next to us is sayin' to Dougie, ''Ave y' not seent bloody fishin' boats they've out theer int bay? 'Ave y' not seen em, 'ave y' not? Bloody hell, what they like love?' he says to his wife, 'What did I say to you when I saw them boats int bay. I said to her, I did, I said them boats, if y' look at the side of 'em ant find name of boatbuilder I'll bet y' a pound to a penny it was Noah. Din't I? I bloody did. Aye.' An' they're all roarin' with laughter. Well I was so ashamed I couldn't keep me mouth shut any longer. 'Excuse me,' I said to the feller on the next table, 'Excuse me. You do watch the Olympic games I take it? And y' do know I suppose that it was the Greeks who invented the Olympic games?' Well they were all lookin' at me. 'Oh yes,' I said, 'they invented a lot of things, the Greeks. In fact,' I said, 'It was the Greeks who were responsible for the most important invention of all – the wheel.' Course I didn't know if it had been invented by the Greeks, the Irish or the Cavemen but I didn't care. Once I'd opened me mouth there was no stoppin' me. 'The English,' I'm goin', 'The English? Don't talk to me about the English, because whilst the Greeks were buildin' roads an' cities an' temples, what were the English doin'? I'll tell y' what the English were doin', they were runnin' round in loin cloths an' ploughin' up the earth with the arse bone of a giraffe.' Well I hadn't meant to get so carried away like that. I suddenly realised how loud I'd been shoutin'. Everyone's lookin' at me – the feller an' his family on the next table have turned away an' Dougie an' Jeanette are sittin' there wonderin' why they asked this lunatic to join them. Well Dougie obviously decides to use diversionary tactics an' he says to the waiter who's just walkin' away. 'Hey mate. What is this?' An' he points to his plate. The waiter says to him, 'Et ees calamares Sir.' 'Yeh but what I'm askin' y',' Dougie says, 'What I'm askin' y', is what is it?' 'Erm . . . eet's calamares, sir, eet's er a type of er . . . feesh.' Well Dougie looks at his plate an' he's not convinced. 'It don't look much like fish to me,' he says. 'My wife's got a very delicate stomach. She's very particular about what she eats. Are you sure this is fish?' 'Sir, I can . . . promees you,' says the waiter, 'eet ees feesh. Eet ees feesh . . . was pulled from the sea thees morning, by my own father. In a boat called 'Noah'.' Well, the silence at our table is deafenin'. We're all sittin' there eatin' an' no-one's sayin' a word. I'm feelin' like a right heel because I've upset them all an' I'm tryin' to think of somethin' to say that'll make it all right. Well y' know what it's like when . . . when there's one of those silences an' you've got to force yourself to find somethin' to say – you always come out with the wrong thing, don't y'? Well what I said was, 'The squid's very nice, isn't it?' The pair of them stopped eatin' an' looked at me. 'Pardon me?' Jeanette said. 'The squid,' I said, pointin' to her

plate, 'The squid, the octopus, it's quite nice really isn' . . .'
Well it was funny the way Jeanette fainted. Y' know sort of in
slow motion. As she comes round I'm tryin' to apologise an'
everythin', but they were off – out – away. They didn't eat in
the hotel after that. Apparently they found this restaurant at
the back of the hotel that does proper Greek food – doner
kebabs. After dinner, whilst everyone else was makin' their way
to the bar, I went up to me room an' grabbed me light coat an'
I walked out of the hotel an' into this lovely night outside.
(*Pause as she remembers it.*) Well that's when I met him. Y' know
. . . Christopher Columbus. That's not his real name. His real
name's Costas. But I call him Christopher. Christopher
Columbus. I'll bet y' don't know why I call him that? It's
because he's got a boat. Well it's his brother's actually. And
because it's er, he, we . . . discovered it. The clitoris. I'm
terrible aren't I? I suppose y' think I'm scandalous – a married
woman, forty-two, got grown up kids. I suppose y' think I'm
wicked. Jane does. 'Shirley,' she said, 'You're acting like a
stupid teenager. I suppose the next thing you're going to tell me
is that the earth trembled?' 'Trembled,' I said, 'Jane, I thought
there'd been an earthquake. It was at least point nine on the
Richter Scale.' 'Oh spare me the details,' she's goin', 'Spare me
the details.' Well she wasn't half jealous. But y' see, it wasn't
my fault; if she hadn't gone off, with the walkin' groin in the
first place – I never would have met Christopher Columbus.
(*Pause.*) He kissed me stretch marks y' know. He did. He said
. . . he said they were lovely . . . because they were a part of
me . . . an' I was lovely. He said . . . he said, stretch marks
weren't to be hidden away – they were to be displayed . . . to
be proud of. He said my stretch marks showed that I was alive,
that I'd survived . . . that they were marks of life. (*Pause.*)
Aren't men full of shit? I mean, can you imagine him, the
mornin' after he's given me this speech – he wakes up an' he
finds his belly has got all these lines runnin' across it? I mean,
can y' see him? Rushin' to the mirror an' goin' 'Fantastic.
Fuckin' fantastic. I've got stretch marks. At last!' But the thing
about him, the thing about Costas was, when he gave y' a load
of guff – *he* believed it. What was marvellous about him was,
he never made y' feel at all threatened. An' he understood how

to talk with a woman. That's the first thing I noticed about him. 'Cos y' know most men, really, they're no good at talkin' with women. They don't know how to listen or they feel that they have to take over the conversation. Like . . . like most fellers, if you said somethin' like . . . like, 'My favourite season is autumn.' Well most fellers'd go, 'Is it? My favourite season's spring. See what I like about spring is that in spring . . .' Then y' get ten minutes of why he likes spring. An' you weren't talkin' about spring – you were talkin' about autumn. So what d' y' do. You end up talkin' about what he wants to talk about. Or you don't talk at all. Or you wind up talkin' to y'self. An' whichever way it works out it always ends up that there's no talkin' goin' on. It just becomes words. Words without meanin'. Words that get spoken . . . but die . . . because they have nowhere to go. But it wasn't like that with Costas. When I came out of the hotel that night I just walked down the little esplanade. There was hardly a soul about, but I noticed the light was on in The Taverna an' outside the front of it there's these tables, with white parasols. Well I'm sittin' there an' he came out to serve me. 'Erm, excuse me,' I said to him, 'I know this sounds a bit soft but would you mind . . . I mean would you object if I moved this table an' chair, over there, by the edge of the sea?' Well he looked at me for a minute. 'You want,' he said, 'You want move table and chair to the sea? What for? You don't like here at my bar?' 'Oh yeh,' I said, 'yeh, it's a lovely bar but, but I've just got this soft little dream about sittin' at a table by the sea.' 'Agh,' he said, an' he smiled. 'A dream, a dream. We move this table to the edge of the sea, it make your dream come true?' 'Erm, yeh,' I said. 'I think so.' 'Then, is no problem. I move the table for you. And tonight when I serve in my bar, I say to customer – tonight, tonight I make someone's dream come true.' Well I thought for a second he was bein' sarcastic – 'cos in England it would have been. But no, he carries the table an' chair over here an' he brings me out this glass of wine I've ordered. Well I paid him an' thanked him but he said to me 'No, I thank you. Enjoy your dream,' then he gave a little bow an' he was gone, back to the taverna, leavin' me alone with the sea an' the sky an' me soft little dream. Well it's funny isn't it, but y' know if you've pictured somethin', you know if you've imagined how somethin's gonna be, made a picture of it in your mind, well it never works out does it? I mean for weeks I'd had this picture of meself, sittin' here, sittin' here, drinkin' wine by the sea; I even knew exactly how I was gonna feel. But when it got to it, it wasn't a bit like that. Because when it got to it I didn't feel at all lovely an' serene. I felt pretty daft actually. A bit stupid an' an' awfully, awfully old. What I kept thinkin' about was how I'd lived such a little life. An' one way or another even that would be over pretty soon. I thought to meself, my life has been a crime really – a crime against God, because . . . I didn't live it fully. I'd allowed myself to live this little life when inside me there was so much. So much more that I could have lived a bigger life with – but it had all gone unused, an' now it would never be. Why. . . why do y' get . . . all this life, when it can't be used? Why . . . why do y' get . . . all these . . . feelin's an' dreams an' hopes if they can't ever be used? That's where Shirley Valentine disappeared to. She got lost in all this unused life. An' that's what I was thinkin', sittin' there on me own, starin' out at the sea, me eyes open wide an' big tears splashin' down from them. I must've sat there for ages because the noise from the hotel bar had died away an' even the feller from the taverna was lockin' up for the night. He came to collect me glass. It was still full. I hadn't even taken a sip. He saw that I was cryin' but he didn't say anythin'. He just sat down there, on the sand and stared out at the sea. An' when I'd got over it, when it was all right to talk, he said, 'Dreams are never in the places we expect them to be.' I just smiled at him. 'Come,' he said, 'I escort you back to your hotel.' An' he did. An' he told me his name was Costas an' I told him my name was Shirley. An' when we got to the front door of the hotel he said to me, 'Tomorrow, you want, to come with me? I take my brother's boat. We go all round the island?' I just shook me head, 'No,' I said, 'It's all right. You've been dead kind as it is. Thank you.' 'Is no problem, I come for you, early.' 'No,' I'm goin', 'Thanks but . . .' 'You afraid?' he suddenly said, 'No,' I said 'but . . .' 'You afraid,' he said, nodding, 'You afraid I make try to foak with you.' I didn't know where to put meself, but he just laughed. 'Of course I like to foak with you. You are lovely

woman. Any man be crazy not to want to foak with you. But I
don't ask to foak. I ask you want to come my brother's boat –
is different thing. Foak is foak, boat is boat. I come fetch you
tomorrow. I bring wine, I bring food and we go. Tomorrow, I
just make you happy. No need to be sad, no need be afraid. I
give my word of honour I don't make try to foak with you.'
Well what could I say? 'Well I'll erm, I'll see y' in the mornin''
then.' Course, the next mornin' I've just got dressed. I'm sittin'
in me room, there's this knockin' on the door, I thought, 'Oh
Christ, he's come up to me room.' Well I opened the door, an'
guess what? Jane's back! 'Shirley, please forgive me. I know I
shouldn't have left you. Shirley, I know I've been awful but
please, please forgive me. I'll make it up to you. Come on, it's
still early, let's go and hire a car and drive out around the
island.' Well what could I do? I mean she had paid for me to
be there. If it hadn't been for Jane I would never have been in
Greece in the first place. She keeps askin' me if I forgive her.
'Of course I forgive y',' I said, an' she threw her arms round me
then. 'Come on,' she said, 'Let's put it all behind us now. Let's
make today the real start of our holiday. I know you've had an
awful time and Shirley I'm sorry. Have you just been sitting
here in your room the past few days? I know you. Without me
being here I suppose you've just been sitting here talking to the
wall, haven't you?' Well I thought to meself, 'How does she see
me? Does she think I'm an old-age pensioner or a five-year-old
child?' 'I'll only be a few minutes,' she's sayin', 'I'll just pick up
a few things from my room.' Well it was just as she got to the
door that there was a knock on it. She pulled it open an' Costas
was there. She took one look at him an' said – 'What is it,
room service? Did you order anything Shirley?' But Costas just
walked straight past her an' into the room. 'Shirley, Shirley,
you come, you come. You late. I wait for you on the quay. I
already put the wine, the food on the boat. I stand I wait an'
then I think, 'Ah, Shirley and me, we get to bed so late last
night, Shirley she must have oversleep.'' Well the look on Jane's
face could've turned the milk. 'Quickly now you get ready.
Don't bring much clothing. I wait on quay for you. Hurry.' An'
as he passes Jane he just goes, 'Apology for interrupting you.
Now you continue cleaning the room.' Well if Jane had kept her

mouth shut, if she hadn't tried to treat me like a child, I might have run after Costas an' said I couldn't go, or could me friend come as well. But she said, 'Shirley. What do you think you're playing at?' I didn't say a word. I just looked at her. She was goin' on about how I'd never been abroad before. When she got to the bit about 'men like that, these Greek islanders who are just waiting for bored middle-aged women to fall into their . . .', I just stormed straight past her an' out. I steered the boat y' know. See me on that bridge – natural. I mean, I knew I wasn't the first woman on that boat an' I certainly wouldn't be the last. But I knew I was with a good man. I knew that whatever happened he wouldn't take anythin' from me. We sailed for miles an' miles. An' we talked. Properly. An' we didn't half laugh. We liked each other. An' isn't it funny, but if you're with someone who likes y', who sort of, approves of y' – well y' like, like start to grow again. Y' move in the right way, say the right thing at the right time. An' you're not eighteen or forty-two or sixty-four. You're just alive. An' I know if I could have seen myself that day I would have said, 'Look at that lovely woman – riding on the sea. Look at that lovely woman, swimming.' Well I know I'd left me swimmin' costume in the hotel. So what? We'd parked the boat an' was lookin' over the side. I said, 'How deep do you think it is here Costas?' 'Mm. Maybe a thousand metres – maybe ten thousand metres, who knows. Maybe so deep it goes on forever.' An' when I stood there, on the edge of the boat, naked as the day I was born, about to jump into this water that was as deep as forever I felt as strong an' as excited an' as bloody mad as I did when I jumped off our roof. The two of us just splashed an' laughed an' swam in the water an' I knew Costas would keep his promise but I didn't want him to because it was the most natural thing in the world. So I swam up to him. An' I put me arms around him an' kissed him. An' that's when I nicknamed him Christopher Columbus. Mind you, I could just as easily have named him André Previn – I don't know where this orchestra came from. Later on, just lyin' there on the boat, with the sun beginnin' to dip towards the evenin', that's when the thought came to me. I tried to like, push it out of me head at first. Because it was too shocking. I kept tryin' to think of other

things, to make this thought go away. But it wouldn't. It was
just there in me head. An' this thought was 'If . . . somehow
. . . if . . . for . . . some . . . reason . . . I . . . didn't . . . go
. . . back . . . home . . . who would really care? Would it cause
anyone any real suffering? Would it damage anyone? Who
would miss – me? Why should I go back? Why should I go back
an' become that woman again when, when that woman isn't
needed anymore. Her job's done. She's brought up her kids. I
mean, they'd say it was awful, it was terrible to have a mother
who went on holiday an' never came back. I hadn't gone round
the pipe. I hadn't. I hadn't fallen in love with Costas. It had
been sweet. It had been lovely. It had been a day full of
kindness. But I hadn't fallen in love with him. I'd fallen in love
with the idea of livin'. An' every day when I woke up, when I
came down here with Jane, when we went an' had a coffee or a
drink at Costas's taverna, when I was lyin' in me bed, just
droppin' off to sleep, it was always there in me head – this
shocking thought – 'I'm not goin' back.' 'I'm not goin' back.'
(*Pause.*) An' of course – all the time I knew really. I knew I'd
have to go back in the end. I knew that I was just one of
millions an' millions before me who'd gone on a holiday an' had
such a good time that they didn't want to go home. Because we
don't do what we want to do. We do what we have to do. An'
pretend it's what we want to do. An' what I wanted to do was
to stay here and be Shirley Valentine. And what I had to do
was to go back there, back to bein' St Joan Of The Fitted
Units. An' all through the days, an' when I said goodbye to
Costas, an' on the way to the airport, an' in the long queue for
the check-in desk I didn't know if I'd do what I wanted to do,
or what I had to do. We were standin' there, in this queue, me
an' Jane an' all the others who had to go back. An' I
remembered this question I was gonna ask Jane. So I said to
her, 'Jane, Jane why is it that there's all this unused life?' She
just said it was because of men, it was all the fault of men, an'
went back to readin' her magazine. An' I thought about it an' I
thought, 'That's rubbish . . . It's not just men who do it to
women. Because I've looked at Joe, an' I know it's the same for
him. He had more life in him than he could use. An' so he
carries all this . . . waste around with him. It's the same for

everyone. I know it. When I'm out when I'm in the shops, when
I see people I grew up with, standin' there in the shop buyin'
vegetables. An' we say how are y' we all say fine an' we
pretend we are because the vegetables are fresh an' we haven't
had a cold this year an' our kids grew up with their limbs intact
an' never got in trouble with the police. We say we're fine. An'
we carry on an' on an' on until we die. An' most of us die . . .
long before we're dead. An' what kills us is the terrible weight
of all this unused life that we carry round.' We'd got to the
check-in desk. Me suitcase was on the conveyor belt with a tag
on it, for England, for home. I stood there, just watchin' it as it
moved away, along the conveyor belt an' through these flaps
an' disappeared into this dark hole. An' I knew then. I knew I
couldn't go with it . . . Jane just called out at first, as she saw
me walkin' away. Then she realised, she knew an' she screamed
at me, to come back, to come back. All the people in the queue
were lookin' at me. An' I knew they all wanted me to 'come
back, come back.' But I just kept walkin', across the concourse.
All I had left was me handbag, the clothes I stood in, Gillian's
robe, me passport an' a few drachmas. An' after I'd paid me
bus fare, even the drachmas had gone. (*Pause.*) When I walked
up to the taverna Costas was talkin' to this woman, sittin' on a
bar stool. As I walked in I heard him sayin' to her: 'You
afraid? You afraid I want make try you . . .' The poor feller,
he nearly dropped his olives when he saw me. 'Don't worry
Costas,' I said, 'I haven't come back for you. I've come back
for the job. The job in your taverna.' Nearly three weeks I've
been workin' there now. I get on well with the customers. Even
the 'Dougies an' Jeanettes', we get a pair of them every week y'
know. They come in, order a drink an', look all dead nervous
at the menu. I always say to them, 'Would you like me to do y'
chips an' egg?' An' they're made up then. Bein' a part of it
here, a proper part of it – it's much better than bein' on
holiday. (*She moves to the table and puts up the parasol.*) I have
most of the days to meself an' just work the nights. I've got the
night off tonight though. Well Joe's arrivin' tonight. The first
time he phoned, y' know after Jane had got back, he screamed
at me. He said I must have finally gone mad. He said I was a
disgrace – to the kids, to him, to meself. It was the easiest thing

in the world to just put the phone down on him. The second time he phoned he said you can't run away from life. I said I agreed with him an' now I'd found some life I had no intention of runnin' away from it. He started to scream an' shout again then; he said he knew all about me 'holiday romance', an' how I'd made a fool of meself but, but if I stopped all this arsin' round, if I got meself home, where I belonged, he said, he said he'd promise never to mention it. I said . . . said . . . 'The only holiday romance I've had, is with meself Joe. An' . . . an' I think . . . I've come to like meself, really.' I said to him, I said, 'I think I'm all right Joe. I think that if . . . if I saw me, I'd say, that woman's O.K. . . . She's alive. She's not remarkable, she's not gonna . . . gonna be there in the history books. But she's . . . she's there in the time she's livin' in. An' certainly she's got her wounds . . . an' her battle scars but maybe, maybe . . . a little bit of the bullshit is true an' an' the wounds shouldn't be hidden away – because, because even the wounds an' the scars are about bein' alive.' There was a long pause. I thought he'd gone off the phone. An' then I heard this voice, 'I knew it,' he was sayin', 'I knew it, it's the bleedin' change of life isn't it?' 'That's right Joe,' I said, 'That's right, it's a change of life. An' that's why you're wastin' your money phonin' me to try an' get me back. I'm not comin' back.' The last time he phoned he said our Brian had been arrested – buskin' without a licence. An' our Millandra was frettin' for me. An' that he loved me an' the only thing he wanted in the world was for me to come back. I explained to him that it was impossible because the woman he wanted to go back didn't exist anymore. An' then I got his letter sayin' he was comin' to get me. To take me back home. Agh God love him, he must've been watchin' Rambo. He'll be here soon. I hope he stays for a while. He needs a holiday. He needs to feel the sun on his skin an' to be in water that's as deep as forever, an' to have his wet head kissed. He needs to stare out to sea. And to understand. (Pause.) I asked Costas if he'd put the table out for me again. He said to me, 'You look for you dream again?' 'No, Costas,' I said. 'No dream. But I'm gonna sit here an' watch for Joe an' as he walks down the esplanade, an' keeps walkin', because he doesn't recognise me anymore, I'll call out to him. An' as he walks back, an' looks at me, all puzzled an' quizzical, I'll say to him – 'Hello. I used to be the mother. I used to be your wife. But now, I'm Shirley Valentine again. Would you like to join me for a drink?'

Blackout

One for the Road

Author's Note
In the rare summer of 1976 I was on holiday on the Isle of Mull where I completed a new stage play. On the title page I typed the words TUPPERWARE MAN, the obvious and perfect title for my new play. Experiencing the twenty-four-hour euphoria I always feel on completion of a play I set off for the village of Dervaig, bought a bottle of claret (or four) in celebration of the completion and called in at the post office. The new script safely despatched to Contact Theatre, Manchester, I selected a fishing rod and a corkscrew and spent the rest of the day on the river bank, ruminating on how for once I had effortlessly come up with the perfect title for a play of mine, and sipping the warm red wine.

Three months later, back home in Liverpool, rehearsals of the play were just about to begin and I received a phone call, from an American lawyer representing the firm of Tupperware. He tells me that his client firm has learnt of the imminent production, has acquired a script and has foreseen one or two 'prahblems'.

It seems that in my play I had suggested that it's not always the easiest thing in the world to fit a Tupperware lid back onto its container. And that didn't go down too well with the firm. I thought I'd better let this guy know that he wasn't dealing with a mere playwright but also with the proud owner of a certificate in 'O' level Law; he was considerably unimpressed although later, when I suggested that in a Court of Law a doddery old judge with shaking hands might also find some difficulty affixing a Tupperware lid to its container he became far more amicable, even saying, 'Mr Russell, I have to confess I have trouble with the goddam lids myself!'

As none of the parties wanted to go to court, least of all the theatre whose production would have to be postponed, we achieved a compromise which, although simple and innocent enough at the time, has since caused me years of headaches. The agreement was that the firm would not press for any changes in the script as long as I was prepared to drop the title. I replaced the phone and went into the kitchen to make a pot of tea and come up with a new title. Eight hours later I was still there, a slightly demented figure amidst the tea cups and sheets of paper.

As the final deadline for a title approached I became desperate and seized upon the idea of taking two incidents from a play with which to make a title. Bill Naughton had written a play called 'Spring and Port Wine'. Well that's a great title I thought, I'll go for that sort of thing. When the theatre's publicist came on the phone I told him that my play was to be called *Painted Veg and Parkinson*.

There was a long pause.

'What!' was the astonished reply when it finally came.

I timidly repeated it, spelt it out for him. During the month's run of the play in Manchester I never heard anyone ever refer to the play by its title; not audience or director or actors. It was always, 'the new play', or 'Willy's play' or 'the play that's on this week'.

After the Manchester production the producer Bob Swash telephoned. 'Willy, I'd love to do that play of yours.'

'Which one?'

'You know, the new one.'

'Painted Veg and Parkinson?'

'Yes. Now look, about the title; we can change it can't we?'

And oh how we tried. Before we went on tour the play was variously known as: *Wagner's Walk, Aerosol Ally, Is Cain Able, Gnomes and Gardens, Phase Two,* and, years before John Wells was to use the same title, *Anyone for Dennis.*

Just before we opened in Norwich we settled on a title which appeared to satisfy all concerned, *Dennis the Menace.* And then we got to Norwich and saw the foyer packed with bodies pushing and shoving to buy tickets. The only problem was that they were young bodies, small bodies, kids – all of whom thought they were buying tickets for a play about Dennis the Menace from the Beano. Adults stayed away in droves for the same simple reason that kids flocked into the theatre. Word was immediately sent to Darlington, our next date – 'Scrap all publicity, new title imminent.'

Imminent? There's optimism! The cast, producer, director and myself spent a long night in a Norwich restaurant throwing possible titles across the table. We were eventually all so weary that when Pru Scales leant across to the next table and wished the object of a birthday party, 'Happy Returns', we mistook it for a suggested title, leapt as one into the air, made a hurried phone call to Darlington, ordered lots more wine and spent the rest of the night celebrating our triumph.

After the tour I had a call from Nottingham Playhouse who wanted to do the play but, yes, they wanted a new title! I suggested they might like to call it *That **/*ing Play*, but they said that might not be too commercial.

Just before the Nottingham production and before the play was published my wife, Annie, walked in one day and said, 'Why don't you call it *One for the Road?*' I gawped at her. It was, after *Tupperware Man*, THE title, perfect. 'But, but, but why didn't you say that months ago, years ago?'

'Oh I did,' she said, quite calmly, 'I said it in Manchester, in Liverpool, in London, in Brighton and Norwich and Darlington, in . . . .'

With the script bearing the title *One for the Road*, I sent the play to the publishers, secure in the certainty that that was the end of all this title business.

Five or six years later driving with Bob Swash, having just agreed to produce *One for the Road* in the West End, we turn to reminiscing about the problems we had with the title some years before I casually observe that we can approach the new production without any title worries. I'm suddenly aware of screeching tyres and the car braking.

I look out of the window to see a theatre where the posters for a new Harold Pinter play are being posted and guess what it's called?

One for the Road was first performed at the Lyric Theatre, London on 21 October 1987, with the following cast:

DENNIS CAIN	Russ Abbott
PAULINE CAIN	Janet Dale
ROGER FULLER	Michael Angelis
JANE FULLER	Elizabeth Bennett

Directed by William Gaunt
Designed by Bruno Santini
Lighting by Mick Hughes

ACT ONE

Before the play begins Joni Mitchell's album, 'Blue', is playing on the stereo.

The stage is a lounge in an 'Executive' dormer bungalow, situated on an estate a few miles from a major northern city. The furnishing is augmented Habitat. The people living here are 'first generation' middle class: their parents still pay rent. Amongst the gadgets and gear there are a dining table and chairs, a video recorder, a stereo unit, a reproduction writing bureau. The set should include a window which looks out onto the back garden. The venetian blind is open and we can see, through the window, roofs of other houses and trees in the distance.

Curtain up on DENNIS – *on the floor by the stereo – he wears headphones –*

We hear, faintly, the sounds he's listening to. Behind DENNIS, *and unseen by him,* PAULINE *enters. She is quite distraught and fails to notice that* DENNIS *is wearing headphones.* PAULINE *pulls out a dining chair and sits.*

PAULINE. I've had enough. From now on . . . that's it. No more, that's it. I will no longer have our child mixing with those Parnes kids, not when he comes out with words like that. I know he gets it from them. They've got mouths like open sewers, those Parnes kids. Well there's going to be a stop to it. I'm not having it. There's enough bad language as it is – on the BBC – without having to put up with it from members of your own family. Well I think it's a disgusting thing for an eleven-year-old child to come out with. What if he comes out with it tonight in front of Roger's kids? You know I've decided not to let him spend the night there after all. When he gets back tomorrow you're going to have to deal with it Dennis. You're going to have a word with John. Dennis? Dennis?

PAULINE *pulls out headphone jack.*

DENNIS *screams and leaps out of his chair, ripping off the headphones.*

You lie there, oblivious, while I'm left to deal with a crisis in the family. Dennis, for God's sake what's wrong with you?

DENNIS. Me ears . . . me ears!

PAULINE. I'm not talking about that – I'm talking about you burying your head in the sand whilst I'm left to cope with one calamity after another.

DENNIS. So what is it now?

PAULINE. What it is Dennis – is that we have a child who has begun to use obscenities.

DENNIS. Such as?

PAULINE. Such as . . . sexual intercourse off.

DENNIS. 'Sexual intercourse off'? Is that what John said?

PAULINE. I think you know very well what he said.

DENNIS. What!

PAULINE. Dennis . . . he swore.

DENNIS. But what did he actually say?

PAULINE. He used a word meaning sexual intercourse.

DENNIS. Which one?

PAULINE. Which one?

DENNIS. Yes, which one?

PAULINE. The worst one.

DENNIS. Fuck?

PAULINE. Dennis!

DENNIS. Because there's loads of words with that meaning. I mean there's . . .

PAULINE. I dare say there are Dennis, but I don't want them spoken in this bungalow . . .

DENNIS. There's shag!

PAULINE. Dennis, Dennis!

DENNIS (as PAULINE *grasps the headphones and clamps them onto her ears*). There's root, screw, legover, knee trembler; there's the old-fashioned style 'roger' and the new one 'bonking'.

PAULINE (*simultaneously*). I'm not listening Dennis. I don't know why you want to behave like this. I don't know what's been wrong with you lately but if you ask me I think you should see a doctor.

DENNIS. I can't think of anymore. Pauline . . . you can take the headphones off now.

PAULINE. I know people get upset when they're approaching their fortieth birthday but quite honestly Dennis I think you're reverting back to childhood.

DENNIS. Pauline . . . it's all right, you can take them off now.

She turns her back on him.

PAULINE. I just don't know what's been wrong with you this past week.

DENNIS. Pauline.

Exasperated he goes to the stereo and plunges up the volume.

PAULINE (*ripping off the cans*). Dennis you swine, you shit.

DENNIS. Aha. So now we know where John's been gettin' this language from.

PAULINE. Dennis I'm warnin' you! In matters of this nature I've always made sure that John knew the correct terms. I've told you, he's getting this language from those Parnes children.

DENNIS. He doesn't get it from the Parnes kids. If a bomb dropped on this estate it'd be the poor bloody Parnes kids who'd get the blame.

PAULINE. Well if he doesn't pick it up from them, you just tell me where he does get it from. I've never heard other children from Phase Two of the estate use language like that.

DENNIS. Pauline, people swear whether they're on Phase One, Phase Two or Phase Three Thousand and Sixty-Nine. People swear everywhere.

PAULINE. They don't Dennis.

DENNIS. They do.

PAULINE. They don't.

DENNIS. They do.

PAULINE. Do they? And when was the last time you heard Sue Lawley say, 'and here's the frigging news.'

DENNIS. All right, I'd forgotten about Sue Lawley.

PAULINE. When we moved to Phase Two I thought we'd be getting away from all that. Well that's it – in future John can stay in with us.

DENNIS. Pauline, he's an eleven-year-old lad. You can't expect him to stay in.

PAULINE. I don't expect him to stay in; he can roam the garden.

DENNIS. 'Roam the garden?' You can't 'roam' a twelve-foot lawn. We have to sunbathe standin' up.

PAULINE. There's a good sixteen-foot lawn out there.

DENNIS. Look, y' can't stop John goin' out. It won't do him any harm.

PAULINE. Oh no, it won't harm an eleven-year-old child if he's subjected to endless filth.

DENNIS. Listen, if you must know . . . I taught him most of the words myself.

PAULINE (*stunned*). You did what?

DENNIS. I had to. I heard him, out in the avenue, tryin' to swear like the rest of them. An' our poor John sounds as though he's swallowed a medical dictionary . . .

PAULINE. Of course . . . because I always taught John the correct terms.

DENNIS. But not when you're supposed to be swearin'. It doesn't have quite the same effect.

PAULINE (*disappearing into kitchen*). All right, OK. You just wait till your mother gets here. You ask her if you should teach her grandchild the correct terms or the obscenities.

DENNIS. I will.

PAULINE. Yes, you do.

DENNIS. 'Now Mother, what do you prefer – cock or penis?' (*Imitating his mother*) 'Well if you don't mind son, I'd rather just have the mixed salad.'

PAULINE (*entering from kitchen*). Anyway, it won't be long now. Their days are numbered, you mark my words.

DENNIS. Whose?

PAULINE. You know very well whose. Whoever it is who's responsible.

DENNIS. For what?

PAULINE. Dennis do you walk around wearing ear-plugs and a blindfold? The whole estate has been up in arms about it since it began.

DENNIS. What?

PAULINE. The attacks Dennis, the attacks. In the last month alone there's been two dozen garden gnomes decapitated. Nearly every fountain and patio waterfall on this estate has been contaminated – with bubble bath; instead of cascading they now do nothing but froth. And what about Shelagh Bennet's Venus De Milo?

DENNIS. What about it?

PAULINE. It's had arms stuck onto it. Only a warped mind could dream up something like that. What terrifies me is who the next victim's going to be. We've escaped so far.

DENNIS. I suppose we have, haven't we?

PAULINE. And fortunately so have Jane and Roger. I think their garden is truly beautiful.

DENNIS. Well no-one'd have a go at their garden would they – I mean who would risk meddlin' with property belongin' to the chairperson of the Ladies' Karate Club? Hey, maybe it's Jane an' Roger who are the culprits.

PAULINE. Dennis don't be stupid – Jane and Roger are the backbone of Phase Two.

DENNIS. But she's always out joggin' isn't she?

PAULINE. What's that got to do with it?

DENNIS. Everythin'. Jane is joggin' along, right? No-one pays any attention to her – It's just Jane the jogger, joggin'. But as she passes some gnome-infested garden she leaps over the wall, pulls out a crowbar from her knickers an' wallop wallop wallop – there's gnomes' heads all over the lawn. When Jane and Roger get here tonight we'll have to be on the lookout for clues – little things like a lump hammer in Jane's handbag an' Radox on Roger's lapel.

PAULINE. Why do you always have to laugh at Jane?

DENNIS. Who's laughin'?

PAULINE. You are Dennis and I'm gettin' fed up with it. When we moved up here to Phase Two Jane could easily have ignored us, pretended she didn't know us. But she didn't do that did she? Jane made sure that we were accepted on Phase Two.

DENNIS. Pauline what is all this Phase Two . . . Look, it's an estate – dormer bungalows, two and three bedroom houses, that's all. It's a housin' estate – not bleedin' Windsor Park.

PAULINE. Oh. I see. I suppose you'd like to go back to living in a terraced house.

DENNIS. As a matter of fact I liked livin' in that terraced house.

PAULINE. As a matter of fact in some ways so did I. But the simple fact is that you received promotion Dennis and executives do not live in terraced houses.

DENNIS. Exec . . . Pauline, I sell central heating.

PAULINE. Yes. But you sell it at an executive level. And it's not central heating you sell. It's Zoned Heating. I'd be grateful if you'd remember that distinction when Jane's here tonight.

DENNIS (*miming holding a microphone and adopting an American film trailer voice, as* PAULINE *exits to kitchen*). Jane! A woman . . . or a legend? Before I met Jane I was just a quivering working-class slob. Before I met Jane I thought lasagne was a Swedish actress, I thought Jane Fonda was a cheese dip, I thought Prunella Scales was a skin disease. In the age before I met Jane . . . No, there was no 'before'.

The telephone rings and DENNIS *answers.*

Hello . . . (PAULINE *enters from kitchen*) Phone box . . . Hello
five oh oh nine . . . Hia Mother . . .

PAULINE. Is that your mother . . . here.

She takes the phone from him. DENNIS *goes into kitchen.*

PAULINE. Mother . . . you were supposed to be getting here
early . . . But I told you to get off at the first bus stop.
(*Covering the receiver and shouting to* DENNIS.) Dennis they've
got lost, they've got off at the wrong bus stop again. Put that
banana back – no, not you Mother. Mother, you've been to the
bungalow God knows how many times, why can't you or Dad
remember where it is? . . . Oh no, they do not all look alike . . .
We do not have a number, Mother, because we do not like to
deface the façade of the bungalow . . . Look, exactly where are
you? . . . Right, now go out of Symphony Square and take the
first right into Sibelius Street. At Elgar Drive, turn right, go
past Mahler Crescent, past Brahms Close till you get to the
Beethoven Underpass. When you come up from the Underpass
you'll see William Tell Avenue right in front of you. . . . That's
right . . . yes . . . You'll see Val's house, you know with the
rather nice Italian wrought iron, that's right. Get up from the
floor – no, not you Mother. That's it and we're right next door
. . . No, no number! . . . just 'The Haven' . . . that's right, The
Haven . . . We'll see you . . . Oh Mother, Mother . . . I'm
cooking Hachis au parmentier tonight – do you think Dad will
like that?

DENNIS *re-enters from the kitchen carrying a can of lager.*

She's just asking him . . . Hello . . . Hello? . . .

She replaces the reciever.

DENNIS. Well? Does he like Hachis au parmentier?

PAULINE. He asked if that was the pebble-dashed semi on the
corner.

DENNIS. Well why didn't you tell her it was cottage pie?

PAULINE. Because Dennis, it is not cottage pie, it is Hachis au parmentier. Oh Dennis, you're not drinking already are you? I don't want you getting drunk. You get loud when you're drunk. Why don't you drink in moderation, like Roger?

DENNIS. Roger? Have you seen the amount Roger gets through?

PAULINE. But he doesn't become loud with it. At least Roger approaches alcohol as an aid to social interaction and not as an aid to lunacy.

DENNIS. But I like lunacy.

PAULINE. All right, but come on, there's lots to do before they arrive. It is for your birthday that we're having this dinner, the least you could do is help get things ready.

DENNIS. What d' y' want doin'?

PAULINE. Bring those chairs in for your mum and dad and have you cleared up that mess in the hall yet?

DENNIS. Which mess?

PAULINE. There's your old haversack lying all over the place.

DENNIS. Rucksack.

PAULINE. You could put that away for a start. I don't know why you got it out in the first place. We're not taking it to Spain with us. You can't get on a shiny new jet with a dirty old rucksack. I don't know why you took it out in the first place.

DENNIS. I took it out because I wanted to look at it and feel it and put me head inside it and smell its smells of diesel oil and grass and Anglesey and beer and Edinburgh and old perfumes and sea salt and sand.

   Pause.

PAULINE (*from kitchen*). And Dennis what are these cans in the bin?

DENNIS (*alarmed*). Which cans?

PAULINE (*from the kitchen*). I don't know, they look like . . . erm, spray cans.

DENNIS (*rushing to hallway*). Oh the erm the . . . er, for the car

. . . got to touch up the er . . . car.

PAULINE *enters from the kitchen. She is looking for something.*

PAULINE. Now where have those table mats disappeared to? (*Thinks.*) Oh, I know . . . (*She goes to the bureau and tries to open it only to find that it is locked.*) Dennis . . . I can't get into the bureau. Dennis I need the table mats. Dennis it's locked.

DENNIS (*re-enters. Stands looking at her*). Erm . . . I know.

PAULINE. Well where's the key?

DENNIS. You want table mats?

He goes to the bureau and opens it whilst concealing its contents.

PAULINE. Dennis, what's in there? Why do you keep it locked? What's in . . .

DENNIS (*handing her the table mats*). Nothing.

PAULINE. Well why keep it locked if . . .

DENNIS. Me poems. I keep me poems in there. I do still write you know.

PAULINE. But why do you keep it locked away?

DENNIS. I keep me poems locked away Pauline. (*Conspiratorial.*) In case someone tries to steal them.

PAULINE (*laughing, relieved*). Oh Dennis . . . (*Embracing him.*) Who'd want to steal your poetry?

DENNIS. Pauline . . . Who'd want to graft arms onto a Venus De Milo?

PAULINE. Do you really still write poems? (*He nods.*) Sometimes I take out your old poems and read them. They make me sad.

DENNIS. Why?

PAULINE. I don't know. Things were just . . . just easier then weren't they? I mean, I know we didn't have the same . . . things then, a car, a beautiful home . . .

DENNIS. Hachis au parmentier, marvellous microwave, digital dishwasher, vacuum cleaner, dimmer switches . . . cordless telephone.

The phone rings, DENNIS *answers it.*

Hello Dad . . .

PAULINE. Oh no . . .

DENNIS. Hello, 54 . . . Hello Dad, that chest's not so good is it?
Go on, take it easy, get y' breath back first . . . That's better,
go on . . . So, exactly where are you now? . . . Erm no, no
that's not exactly nearer . . . erm, it sounds to me as though
you've wandered into the adjoining estate . . . Yeh . . . yeh I
know they all look alike . . . Listen, have you found that little
pub on the corner? That's right, The Crotchet and Quaver . . .
Well go up the pedestrian precinct. (*Spelling it out.*) Pedestrian
precinct . . . The street, go up the street . . . Listen it'd be
much easier if y' just let me pick y' up in the car . . . yes, I
know me mother gets indigestion if she has to travel in a car
. . . Well look . . . just, just get back onto the other side of the
road and follow the instructions Pauline gave you . . . all right,
OK we might see y' by next Christmas then? Tarar.

PAULINE. Dennis, what are we going to do? I wanted to have
them here early so that we could get them settled in before Jane
and Roger arrive. What are we going to do?

DENNIS. Just pray that they turn back before they reach the
Pennines.

PAULINE *exits to kitchen and* DENNIS *puts on a record at low
volume.*

PAULINE. You know how Jane always casts a critical eye on
things. Dennis have you opened the wine yet?

DENNIS. What for? There's no-one here yet.

PAULINE. Dennis what is wrong with you? Surely you've learnt
by now that wine needs time to breathe.

DENNIS. Breathe? It's Italian plonk on special offer. That lot
wouldn't breathe if it was in an oxygen tent.

PAULINE. What's wrong with you? You've been in this mood all
day haven't you?
He stares at her.
Ah I'm sorry if I'm moaning at you Dennis but you won't take

anything seriously. Tomorrow Den, you'll be forty years of age. I mean, I used to laugh at your antics as much as anyone when we were young. But we're not young any longer Den. You're not a youth anymore. But you're still acting as if you were. Dennis you've got responsibilities – you're a mortgagee, you're a father, you're a British Gas Shareholder.

She looks at him and realises that he hasn't been listening to a word.

Dennis are you listening to me?

He merely stares, absorbed.

Dennis, I'm taking time off from the kitchen to talk to you and you're not even listening to . . .

DENNIS. Listen.

PAULINE. What?

DENNIS. Listen . . . Listen to that.

PAULINE. Listen to what Dennis?
He goes to the stereo and replaces needle on track. He turns up the volume and we listen to the verse before he turns the volume down again.

DENNIS (*reciting the verse we have just heard*).
Richard got married to a figure skater
An' he bought her a dishwasher and a coffee percolator
And he drinks at home now, most nights
With the TV on
And all the house lights left up bright.

PAULINE. Well?

DENNIS. That's me.

PAULINE. Who?

DENNIS. Richard.

PAULINE. But you're Dennis.

DENNIS. And Richard. You're the figure skater.

PAULINE. Well I hope I never have to prove it. I can't even stand up on roller skates.

DENNIS. Richard. That is me, isn't it?

PAULINE. Dennis I don't know what you're going on about. (*Returning to kitchen.*) But if you're going to change your name it's not going to be Richard. I'm not having people rushing round this bungalow shouting out 'Dick'.

DENNIS (*more to himself than* PAULINE). The song . . . it's about a feller who used to drink in the bars. And the girl loved him but . . . for some reason they went their separate ways until years later when they run into each other again. And the feller, Richard, who used to drink in the bars with his crowd and talk and talk and talk, about what him and the rest of them were going to do, where they were going to go, well . . . he hasn't done any of it. He hasn't gone anywhere. When the girl knew him, they'd all been young and where they were all headed to was somewhere good and alive and continuing. But when the girl meets him again . . . He doesn't drink in the bars now. He just goes down to the corner and gets a six pack and takes it back home. He drinks it with the telly flickering before him and all the house lights turned up bright.

PAULINE. What happens to the girl?

DENNIS. It . . . it doesn't say. It's about him, the song, not the girl.

PAULINE. Ah yeh, but it's all right for him, isn't it?

DENNIS. Why?

PAULINE. Well, I mean, he's settled down hasn't he? He's got a house and everything. But what's the girl ended up with? Is she married?

DENNIS. I don't know.

PAULINE. Yeh. See what I mean. Hey Den, why don't you play your guitar these days? Mm? I used to like it when you gave us a song. Why don't you play it anymore?

DENNIS. Hey, maybe I will. I could get it out the garage tonight, put some new strings on it . . .

PAULINE. Agh not tonight Dennis. Not when we've got people coming. Put a record on if you want some music. Let's have

something classical – let's have some James Galway.
(DENNIS's *reaction*.) No, perhaps you're right. Classical might
be a bit heavy for a Saturday. Oh Dennis, put John Denver on.
Nobody could take exception to John Denver.

DENNIS. I could. I hate John Denver.

PAULINE. Dennis, you love John Denver.

DENNIS. I do not. I have got a glorious loathing of John Denver.

PAULINE. Well you used to like him. You used to try and comb
your hair to look like John Denver's.

DENNIS. Pauline, I'd prefer to have any head of hair in the
world other than John Denver's – I would rather have hair like
Arthur Scargill than John Denver.

PAULINE. But you used to be so fond of John Denver.

DENNIS. Well, now I hate him.

PAULINE. Dennis don't keep saying 'hate'. If you don't like him
you could at least say 'detest'.

DENNIS. But I don't 'detest' him.

PAULINE. I told you.

DENNIS. I 'hate' him. Hate, hate, hate, hate, hate.

PAULINE. You carry on like that and you'll have Val next door
hearing you. She's devoted to John Denver.

DENNIS (*goes to window. Opens it and shouts out*). I, Dennis Cain,
of The Haven wish it to be known that I have a passionate and
terrible hatred of John, Goldilocks, Denver.

> PAULINE *begins to struggle with him to get him away from the
> window.*

John Denver should be garrotted with his own G string and . . .

> *She finally manages to pull him away.*

PAULINE. Dennis. Have you gone mad? What are you trying to
do? Shouting stuff like that . . . My God, don't you realise how
many people you could upset? John Denver's very well thought
of on this estate. (*As she closes the window.*) Oh no . . . there's
Val. Hello Val. Yes I thought I heard someone shouting too.

That's why we were looking out. I think it came from your side Val . . .

DENNIS. Definitely your side Val.

PAULINE. Ah yeh, that's true, it probably was them. You know what they're like, those Parnes kids.

DENNIS. They want throttlin' Val.

PAULINE. I'll have some strong words for them when I see them again . . . OK Val. Bye.

DENNIS. Bye Val. Y' know, you could get to feel very sorry for those poor bloody Parnes kids.

PAULINE. Well, what do you expect me to do? Tell her the truth? Oh don't worry Val, it was just Dennis treating the estate to his opinion of John Denver. Well I hope for your sake that Roger and Jane didn't hear you. John Denver's a God in their eyes.

The telephone rings.

Dennis, you get it. Look at the time and I'm not even changed yet.

She goes out as DENNIS *picks up the telephone.*

DENNIS. Hello, Control Tower . . . No, it's me Mother. Dennis your son. Control Tower? It was a joke. Well . . . I know it's nothing to laugh at . . . Well if you'd let me pick you up in the car . . . I know you get indigestion in cars . . . yes I know everywhere looks the same on these estates . . . Mother, you're lucky, a woman went out for a loaf of bread once an' was gone for six months. Well it would be stale. Look, did you find the Crotchet and Quaver? That's were you're phoning from? You found the underpass? Right, look . . . Get someone to direct you to the hypermarket. Supermarket – its a big shop and you'll see a phone there. Ask the barman. Telephone when you get there an' I'll fetch the car for you . . . No Mother, you won't have to travel in the car if you don't want to . . . I'll drive very slowly and you an' me Dad can follow the tail lights . . .

The door chimes play a snatch of the William Tell Overture.

I'll have to go Mother, the Lone Ranger's at the door. Tarar.
Good luck.

DENNIS *exits to front door. From off we hear.*

Aye aye.

ROGER. All right kid.

JANE. Evening Dennis.

DENNIS *enters followed by* JANE *and* ROGER. ROGER *is
carrying a bottle of wine.*

DENNIS. Come in. Come in. Pauline's just gettin' changed.

JANE. Not ready when her guests arrive? A little black mark for
Pauline.

ROGER. Black mark for herself, eh?

JANE. It's a good thing you're entertaining us and not some of
the others I could think of on this estate. You know that some
people would hold a mistake like that against you for life.

DENNIS. Jane, that very thought crossed my mind as I opened
the door – I said to myself, self I said how lucky we are that
tonight it's only good old ordinary Jane and Roger!

ROGER (*handing* DENNIS *the wine*). There y' go kid. Brought y'
a little bottle of somethin'.

DENNIS. Ta Rodge. Red. I'll put it by the cooker to keep warm.

JANE. Warm? Dennis, that is Beaujolais Nouveau. I thought
everybody knew that Beaujolais is the one red wine which must
be served chilled.

DENNIS. Oh, of course, trust me. Chilled it must be. Well Jane,
I'm sure, if you held onto it for half an hour . . .!

ROGER. It's the only red wine we drink in summer. Isn't it love?
You know what they say about red wine in summer don't you
kid? 'In summer, big bold burgundies should be abandoned.'

DENNIS. I shun them Rodge!

ROGER (*producing a box-like, wrapped object*). Now kid, bought
y' a little pressy. Here. You'll love it. He'll love it won't he?

DENNIS. Thanks Rodge, ta Jane.

He begins to unwrap it.

JANE. Mum and Dad not here yet Dennis? I was just saying to Roger, it must be years since I saw them.

DENNIS. It might be years still.

He unwraps the gift to reveal a record-carrying case.

Ogh, thanks. A record-carrying case.

JANE. Look inside Dennis.

DENNIS (*lifting the lid*). Oh. (*Without enthusiasm.*) A record as well.

ROGER. You'll never guess who it's by kid.

DENNIS. I think I might just Rodge.

JANE. Well there's no need to guess Dennis – just take it out and have a look.

DENNIS. Do I have to?

JANE. Not if you don't want to see your present.

ROGER. He's just savourin' the moment, aren't y' kid?

DENNIS. Yeh.

ROGER. Well . . . go on, go on.

DENNIS (*pulling out the record*). John Denver.

ROGER. It's the double album y' know kid, the megamix that is. Take y' two hours to get through that.

DENNIS. Fabulous. two hours!

PAULINE *enters.*

PAULINE. Hello everyone.

DENNIS. Hello Pauline!

ROGER. Ogh . . . Now look at that. You look great kidder. Doesn't she look magic?

JANE. That's a lovely little dress Pauline.

PAULINE. Thank you Jane. Oh Dennis, what's that?

DENNIS. It's a present, from Jane and Roger.

PAULINE. Ogh . . . a record-carrying case. Isn't that lovely.
When you go out you'll be able to take all your records with
you.

DENNIS. Take them for a walk.

PAULINE. Ogh, and a record as well. What is it? (*She takes out
the record, see what it is, drops it back and slams the case shut.*)
No-one's got a drink. Who'd like a drink? Dennis what are you
doing not offering our guests a drink?

JANE (*laughing*). Another black mark Dennis.

DENNIS. Another one. If we carry on like this it'll be the firing
squad for us won't it? Lined up at dawn, in Sainsbury's car
park an' shot by a platoon of the finest hostesses on the estate.

PAULINE. Dennis, will you please offer Jane and Roger a drink?

DENNIS. Ah . . . but, my love, it seems that when I purchased
the said red I was forgetting that 'in summer big bold
burgundies should be abandoned.' Trust me to forget that.
That's obviously why it was on special offer. Everyone else on
the estate knows of the summer burgundy curse, but not me. I
rush in and buy up seventeen friggin' litres of the stuff. Well, at
least there'll be something to look forward to when winter
comes. That's if we last that long, now that we've got seventy-
nine black marks in the book and an evening of desperate
sobriety ahead. Tell me Jane what do you prefer, cock or penis?

PAULINE. Dennis!

JANE. Oh don't worry Pauline. I'm used to him. Anyway, he
can't fool me – I know there are no such wines on the market.

ROGER. Anyway kid, we don't mind drinkin' red. I mean, we're
not exactly connoisseurs. What we said about the burgundies,
we just read it in the paper last Sunday.

JANE. I didn't read it in the paper.

ROGER. We did love.

JANE (*an Exocet glance*). Roger, you may well have done. But I
did not. For as long as I can remember, I have known about

the big bold burgundies.

ROGER. I remember . . .

JANE. Roger!

DENNIS (*miming a karate chop*). Watch it Rodge.

JANE. Anyway, don't you think there are more important matters than wine to discuss?

ROGER. Oh aye. I'd forgotten.

PAULINE. What is it? Jane what's wrong?

JANE. My God, is nothing sacred? Are we all to be brought down by the times in which we live? Are we all to be victims of this sickness?

PAULINE. Jane . . .?

JANE. It's wicked. It's mindless.

PAULINE. What's happened?

DENNIS. What's up then flower?

ROGER. Don't push her kid. She's had a shock. We both have.

JANE. I don't really know if I can bear to talk about it.

ROGER. Woke up this mornin', what did we find? The whole of our garden . . .

JANE. Defiled!

PAULINE. Oh Jane, no.

ROGER. Defiled kidder. Same pattern; gnomes' heads all over the place. Ornamental pool looks more like a soddin' jacuzzi.

JANE. But no only that. Tell them Roger, tell them about the vegetables.

ROGER. Y' know my cabbages Dennis? Them with the lovely little hearts in them? Everyone of them, covered in paint.

PAULINE. Oh no!

JANE. Pauline you haven't heard the half of it. They weren't just painted at random, were they Roger?

ROGER. They were not. Not content with mere vandalism, the

perpetrators decided to show off their artistic talent at the same time – those grand little cabbage hearts had been deliberately painted to look like . . . like . . . well, I'll be frank, like breasts.

PAULINE. Oh that's terrible.

ROGER. For the sake of decency I'll not tell y' what they did to my organic cucumbers.

PAULINE. Have you lost all your little organic vegetables Roger?

ROGER. Oh no. They'll still grow. But that's not the point is it? I mean what are we gonna do when we have people round to dinner? You know our dining table faces the garden. We've often sat there, with guests, haven't we love, lingering over a coffee and admiring the vegetables. But what we gonna do now? Ey? We can hardly have our bloody guests starin' out at a row of tits an' pricks can we?

JANE. Roger! Language please.

ROGER. Well . . . we're all adults. Anyway, it makes y' swear.

JANE. I suppose from now on we'll just have to eat with the blinds closed.

DENNIS. Couldn't you just move your dining table?

ROGER. We will not move our dining table. That's the one thing they want us to do kid. They'd like to see us move our dining room table because that would show we'd given in to them. An' if we do that – we've lost. No kid, when you're faced with terrorism you stand firm. I will sit where I've always sat, at my dining room table. I'll defy them.

DENNIS. An' who is 'them' Rodge?

JANE. Dennis, I would have thought that was patently obvious. It's those Parnes children isn't it?

DENNIS. The Parnes kids? Why the poor bloody Parnes kids?

JANE. Dennis we know you don't take a great deal of interest in the community life of this estate but some of us do and naturally we learn things about our neighbours. Mr Parnes, you know what he is don't you?

DENNIS. What?

JANE. Tell him Roger. An art teacher. An art teacher Dennis, that's what. An art teacher.

ROGER. See kid, see . . .

DENNIS. But that doesn't mean . . .

JANE. And Mrs Parnes . . . have you seen her, have you Pauline?

JANE. Who? Mrs?

DENNIS. What's wrong with her?

JANE. Dennis, Dennis. She wears wellingtons.

DENNIS. So?

JANE. In summer Dennis! And she always wears that CND badge.

DENNIS. Well? You used to wear a CND badge, years ago.

JANE. Dennis that was quite different. When we did it we did it because it was fun. It's not the same today.

DENNIS. But that doesn't mean . . .

JANE. I'm afraid I think it does Dennis.

ROGER. Anarchists, all of them. A paint brush in one hand, an aerosol can in the other.

PAULINE. A what?

DENNIS. Anyone like a drink?

ROGER. An aerosol can, trademark of the vandal.

DENNIS. Big bold burgundies all round eh? I know it's summer an' all that but if we use our imagination an' pretend it's winter we might just be able to pour a gallon or two down our throats.

ROGER. One of the worst things about this vandalism is I have to admit they did a good job. I was fumin' when I saw that garden of mine. But even so, the artistic side of me told me that it was very well executed. Those cabbage hearts have got recognisable nipples on them.

JANE. And that's what's so distressing about this particular wave of vandalism. It's not ordinary vandalism; there's something ominously . . . creative about it.

DENNIS *pours wine.*

DENNIS. Obnoxious little aroma Jane –

JANE. It's very dry –
ALL cheers!

DENNIS (*proposing a toast*). The Parnes kids.

ROGER. They'll not get my greenhouse though.

DENNIS. Have you taken it down then Rodge?

ROGER. I've not taken it down, and I will not be taking it down.
But whoever wants to get at my greenhouse is gonna have to get
over a six foot fence with barbed wire on top. The only way
you'd get at my greenhouse now is from the air an' I reckon
even those Parnes kids haven't got recourse to a helicopter.

JANE. And of course after tomorrow, they'll have the force to
cope with.

PAULINE. The police force?

JANE. The Residents' Force Pauline. I've told Roger it's the only
way. He's organised a meeting for tomorrow – haven't you
Roger?

ROGER. Well, as I said love, there's no point rushin' into things.

JANE. The meeting is at our house.

ROGER. 'Cos there's all sorts of problems that have to be sorted
out.

JANE. At two-thirty.

ROGER. Half-two the meetin' is. You will be there won't y' Den?

JANE. Of course Dennis will be there. We know that in the past
Dennis has avoided joining any of our clubs or committees. But
that was in a time of peace. In war it's different, isn't it
Dennis? At a time of crisis we band together, don't we? We
unite to protect what is ours. Don't we?

DENNIS *remains dumb.*

Unless, that is, we happen to be some sort of a freak.

ROGER. KCC the movement is to be called. Keep Castlehills

Cool. I thought of that. I reckon it could be a good thing for Phase Two residents to get involved in somethin' like this. There's lots of chaps I meet who are bored rigid an' somethin' like this could be a Godsend to them. I reckon it could catch on in a big way; the possibilities are endless. If we really got it organised we could offer all sorts of facilities – diving instruction, swimmin' . . .

DENNIS. Commando trainin' in the park, SAS classes, torture techniques . . .

ROGER. We could even have a junior section – get the kids involved.

JANE. Roger we're forming a protection force, not a youth club.

ROGER. Yeh, but I think it'd be a good idea to get the kids involved, especially the likes of the Parnes kids. We'll need somebody to design and draw leaflets an' posters. Now if the Parnes kids' artistic talents were channelled in this way maybe they wouldn't need to resort to vandalism.

JANE. Roger, what is the point of having a movement like KCC if all the vandals are brought into it?

ROGER. Well the . . .

JANE. No, some of the vandals must be kept on the outside.

ROGER. Yeh but . . .

PAULINE. Dennis where have your parents got to?

DENNIS. Bombay? Karakas? No they've probably just been arrested by one of Roger's special task force. They're probably bein' interrogated right this minute: 'Vat ees zee purpose of zees meesteerious phone calls? Vat ees meant by z Haven? Who ees zees agent you call hachis au parmentier?'

PAULINE. If they're not here soon Dennis the hachis au parmentier will be . . .

JANE. Oh have you prepared hachis au parmentier Pauline? Aren't you brave? Isn't Pauline adventurous Roger? Can we have a little look?

PAULINE *and* JANE *exit to the kitchen.*

ROGER. Hachis what?

DENNIS. Cottage pie – no problem. Come here, listen to this.

They go to the stereo.

ROGER. New album kid?

DENNIS. Not really. Listen.

DENNIS *plays him the verse from 'Last Time I Saw Richard'.*

ROGER. Joni Mitchell?

DENNIS. Yeh, but did you hear what she said?

ROGER. What was that he bought for her?

DENNIS. A dishwasher an' a coffee percolator. Rodge, that's me.

ROGER. Now let me get this right; you have bought Pauline a dishwasher?

DENNIS. No. The feller in the song. It's me!

ROGER. Is that right kid?

DENNIS. Do you know what I did today?

ROGER. If your Saturday was anythin' like mine you probably spent most of it pushin' a wire trolley round the hypermarket tellin' yourself that at any minute you'll be approached by some tantalisin' an' uninhibited feminist who'll recognise immediately your dedication to sexual equality by virtue of the fact that you know your way round the store and thus must always do the shopping. Turned on to unknown heights by the discovery of a truly non-sexist male she will insist on having you there and then amidst the bin bags and frozen pizzas.

DENNIS. No.

ROGER. No it didn't happen to me either but you've got to think of somethin' when you're doin' the bloody shoppin'.

DENNIS. Roger, what I did was . . . I was out in the car . . . I had to go past the motorway sliproad. An' I saw them all – people, fellers, women, with rucksacks, sleepin' rolls, lined up at the side of the road, hitchin' a lift, goin' away. I pulled in an' parked an' just sat an' watched them as they got lifts, one by one, each of them goin', movin' on, away, anywhere. Rodge,

I wanted to get out of my car, leave it behind an' take my place in the queue of hitch-hikers.

ROGER. What the bloody hell for?

DENNIS. Tomorrow Rodge – I'll be forty. Forty. Remember Rodge, years ago, what we all said we were gonna do? Don't you remember the nights, sittin' listenin' to Dylan, plannin' how we were gonna spend our lives.

ROGER. Agh . . . we've not done so bad Dennis.

DENNIS. But what we were gonna do Rodge – the promises we made. You were gonna be a famous singer Rodge.

ROGER. Well . . . that was years ago. I was gonna do everythin' then. Me? I was gonna light up the world I was. But there's no point dwellin' on all that. I've got a good life here. No point allowin' yourself to get dissatisfied. I mean nobody's ever really satisfied Den. Look at someone like, like Paul Simon say. Paul Simon, right, he's got money, sold hundreds of millions of records, albums at the top of the charts, packed concerts in Wembley, Central Park – but is he happy? Is he hell. An' y' know why? When he goes to bed at night he doesn't lie there thinking' – I'm Paul Simon, money, records, concerts, huge. He lies there thinkin' 'I'm Paul Simon – midget.' He's small y' see Dennis an' he'll never be satisfied. What Paul Simon really wanted to be y' see, was Garfunkel. He wanted to be tall. But that he'll never be.

DENNIS. But Roger, when I moved to Phase Two I never expected to find you here Rodge.

ROGER. You're gettin' it all wrong Dennis. I could sing a song all right but I was only average.

DENNIS. Roger you were good. Everyone said you could have made it.

ROGER. Nah . . .

DENNIS. You could.

ROGER. I know. (*Pause.*) I tell the kids y' know – I tell our Michael an' Amanda. 'You think,' I say to them, 'You think I'm just some feller who sells double glazin' an' mows the lawn.

But your father,' I say, 'your father could have been a great singer, a famous man.' Mind you Dennis, I say 'could,' but who knows, one day I might still do it.

DENNIS. You won't Rodge. None of us will.

ROGER. How do you know?

DENNIS. You won't Rodge. It's too late. You've given up.

ROGER. Says who?

DENNIS. Says me.

ROGER. Well you're wrong kid. You're bloody wrong.

DENNIS. Am I Rodge?

ROGER (*rattled*). Of course you are. Listen, if I've given up then how come I always take the part of a famous singer when we're playin' Wogan?

DENNIS. When you're doin' what?

ROGER. Playin' Wogan – you know what I mean.

DENNIS. I don't.

ROGER. You mean y' never play the Wogan game?

DENNIS. No.

ROGER. See. You think you know everythin' but when it comes down to it kid you're right out of bloody touch. Wogan. They all do it round here – it's the in thing.

DENNIS. Well what is it you do for Christ's sake?

ROGER. Y' play out the interview don't y'? Like, when me an' Jane play it she takes the part of Wogan an' I play the part of me, when I'm famous. Some of them round here play 'Russell Harty' but I don't think it's as good. Look, come on, I'll show y'. Right, now that's Terry's chair, there. Now you sit there an' you be him, you be Terry Wogan. Right, come on Terry, come on Wogie, come on . . .

> DENNIS *sits, bewildered, in the 'Wogan' chair.*
> ROGER *moves to the side of the room, ready to make his entrance. He vocally improvises the 'Wogan' theme music, and provides a roar of applause.*

DENNIS. What do I do?

ROGER. Be him. Be him. Right . . .

DENNIS. You and Jane do this?

ROGER. I've told y' everyone does it.

DENNIS. In your front room?

ROGER. Of course. Now come on kid, be him . . . be Terry.

> ROGER *again improvises the introductory music.*
> DENNIS *faces front and adjusts himself to face the studio audience.*

DENNIS. Hello and welcome. On my show tonight, a man who has risen from the depths of nowhere to find himself where he is today – at the pinnacle, the very pinnacle of the entertainment industry.

ROGER. That's it kid . . . great, great.

DENNIS. He's a fellow who has won not only the love of the public, but also the respect of his colleagues in the world of show business. A real clever dick. An international star, a world celebrity . . . in short, a superstar.

ROGER. Ogh wonderful kid. You're a natural.

DENNIS. A rare phenomenon. A creature unique in the annals of show business.

> ROGER *is preening himself.*

But my first guest tonight . . .

> ROGER *stung.*

Is Roger Fuller.

ROGER. Now look here Dennis . . .

DENNIS. Come on, you're on, you're on . . .

> ROGER *makes his entrance, providing his own signature tune and applause.*

DENNIS. Welcome . . . welcome. Roger, I believe congratulations are due to you in respect of your latest sell-out concert at New York's Madison Square Garden, where I hear you were joined on stage by John Denver.

ROGER. That's right Terry. John just called me up the day of the concert an' we were chewin' a little fat y' know an' . . .

DENNIS. 'Scuse me, excuse me – You were chewing a little fat what?

ROGER. Y' what?

DENNIS. It was a joke. 'A little fat what?'

ROGER. Look kid, I do the jokes. When Jane plays Wogan she plays Wogan without the jokes. I get the jokes.

DENNIS. Now Roger, you were tellin' us about Madison Sq . . .

ROGER. Well it's like I was tellin' y' Terry, John called me up an' he knew about my concert an' he said it would be a great privilege for him if he could join me onstage. You know he's doin' an album of my songs in the fall?

DENNIS. No I didn't know that Roger. I'll have to look out for it.

ROGER. Yeh John and me we been . . .

DENNIS. Yes, we'll come back to that a little later. Erm, for the moment I'd like to put to you a question that I know most of my viewers would like an answer to, and it's this, Roger, in your line of business, do you get a lot of women to screw?

ROGER. Ey, hold on, hold on. Wogan wouldn't ask a question like that.

DENNIS. He'd want to though.

ROGER. He might want to. But he wouldn't bloody do it on the air.

DENNIS ('to audience'). Do you know I don't think he's goin' to answer the question.

ROGER. I can't answer that. Ask proper Wogan questions.

DENNIS. OK, OK. Let's go back to that concert.

ROGER. That's more like it. That's it kid. Go on.

DENNIS. Now a little birdie told me that when Denver came on stage he was greeted with most of the audience walking out in protest.

ROGER. That's not true.

DENNIS. And this little birdie went on to say that when you started to sing together the remainder of the audience walked out as well.

ROGER. Hold on, hold on.

DENNIS. And that Denver and yourself ended up singing to the usherettes, all of whom were fast asleep by the end of the show.

ROGER. I don't have to put up with this. I'm leaving.

DENNIS. I'm sorry to insist on this but . . .

ROGER. Y' know what you are don't y? Y' just a bog Irish pillock who knows sod all about nowt. Russell Harty could knock you sideways.

DENNIS. Agh come on Rodge, I was just gettin' into it then.

ROGER. No, I've had enough. You're no good. You'll never get the hang of it kid. You've got to understand the personality of the man before you can do it justice.

DENNIS. Ah Rodge, come on, it's good this . . .

JANE *enters with more drinks.*

JANE. What's going on here?

{ DENNIS. It's him.
   ROGER. It's him. I'm tryin' to teach him how to play the Wogan game but he's useless. He'll never get it.

JANE. The Wogan game?

ROGER. Wogan, the game we play.

JANE. Oh. That silly game you sometimes play with the children.

PAULINE *enters.*

PAULINE. Dennis where are your parents? If they're not here soon the dinner's going to be ruined.

DENNIS. Just leave it in the oven.

JANE. Dennis, there are some dishes which will survive a spell in the oven but I'm afraid hachis au parmentier is not one of them.

DENNIS. But if they haven't arrived, they haven't arrived.

PAULINE. But it's not fair Dennis, they're always doing this.

DENNIS. All right, all right . . . I'll get the car out and see if I can find them.

ROGER. Want me to come with you kid? Case y' meet any hitch-hikers?

DENNIS. No, you stay near the phone Rodge. If Wogan rings, tell him I'm only available Tuesday and Thursday.

  DENNIS *exits*.

ROGER. Mind if I help meself to another big bold burgundy kidder?

PAULINE. I'll get it for . . .

ROGER. No y' won't pet. You sit there. I'm a liberated man I am y' know. You'll not see me sittin' around expectin' women to wait upon me hand and foot, will you Jane?

JANE. Roger just go and get your drink please.

DENNIS. If I'm not back in three weeks send the tracker dogs.

ROGER. I have beaten the two big 'C's of our time Pauline, chauvinism . . . and cholesterol.

  He makes his exit to the kitchen.

PAULINE. I do like Roger. (*Pause.*) I mean, as a friend.

JANE. Doesn't everybody Pauline. He's a very popular man.

PAULINE. He's always in demand isn't he?

JANE. Always Pauline. I think it's his natural magnetism that so many people respond to. And his strength, this . . . inner strength which seems, somehow, to communicate itself to those around him.

PAULINE. And you're very happy together aren't you?

JANE. Intensely Pauline. And you know the main reason for that don't you? I know it's basic, but it's true – Sex, Pauline, sex. Roger and I have a wonderful sex life.

PAULINE. Oh. Erm . . . good.

JANE. You see Pauline, when it somes to sex, most couples make one basic mistake – they leave it to chance – nothing is organised. You see what I mean?

PAULINE. Well I think . . .

JANE. You see, couples organise their . . . kitchens don't they? Their kitchens, their gardens, their cars, their jobs – all organised but when it comes to sex, what happens?

PAULINE. What Jane?

JANE. No forward planning! Everything's improvised, it's all spur of the moment stuff. And that is fatal.

PAULINE. Is it?

JANE. Pauline. What sort of a kitchen do you think you'd have if it had not been planned and organised in advance, what sort of garden? My God, just think what sort of roads we'd have if things weren't organised – instead of everybody efficiently driving along on the left you'd just have people banging into each other all over the place.

PAULINE. Yes I suppose you would.

JANE. There's no suppose about it Pauline. And that's why, in our lovemaking, Roger and I leave nothing to chance. We've eliminated the variables Pauline and achieved sex – with structure.

She beams, proud.

JANE. Now don't get me wrong – Roger is a ram. Yes.

PAULINE. Oh.

JANE. Very demanding Pauline. Very. He's lusty. A big lusty man.

ROGER *enters, bearing a glass brimming with red wine.*

ROGER. 'Ey, it's good stuff this kidder. Y' get the taste after a few.

JANE. Roger!

ROGER. What?

JANE (*indicating that he should get out but he fails to catch on*). Roger! How many times have I told you that when drinking wine you have to leave room in the glass for the bouquet?

ROGER. Ah. (*He swallows the drink in one.*) Done. (*He sniffs the glass.*) There. A lovely bouquet.

JANE. Roger go and see how the dinner's getting on.

ROGER. Eh?

JANE. Roger. Get out.

ROGER. Oh . . . Oh . . . (*He exits to kitchen.*)

JANE. Shelagh's asked me if I'll give a series of talks on the subject beginning in September.

PAULINE. What subject?

JANE. Sex. Of course it means I'll have to give up the karate club but, well, I don't think there's much left for me to learn in karate. And if I can help the sexual sufferers in this community then I think it's my duty to do so.

PAULINE. That's very good of you Jane.

JANE. Each talk will last about an hour an' then of course I'll take questions. But September could be too late for you, couldn't it Pauline?

PAULINE. Pardon Jane?

JANE. Pauline, Pauline, you can't afford to be reticent. If you are going to solve your problems one of the first things you're going to have to do is learn how to talk freely about them.

PAULINE. Jane, which problems?

JANE. You poor love. God, what you must be suffering.

PAULINE. Jane what do you . . .

JANE. Reading is highly important. Not pornography but material written by people with expert medical knowledge, authentic sexologists. The problems that you and Dennis are facing alone can be beaten with a friend at hand. Premature is he? Premature? Far more common than you'd think Pauline.

PAULINE. No Jane. Dennis was carried for the full nine months.

JANE. As common as the common cold but the cause of far greater misery. But it can be cured Pauline, simply. In some cases it's merely a question of underpants.

PAULINE. Pardon?

JANE. Yes. Underpants! I'll bet he wears them extremely tight, doesn't he Pauline, doesn't he? Tight, around the crotch, jockey style, displaying his outlines. Am I right Pauline? Of course I'm right. You see, it's unnatural for them to be so hemmed in Pauline. Get him into boxer shorts Pauline, and your problem could be solved.

PAULINE. But . . . Jane, we haven't got a sexual problem.

JANE (*laughs*). The marrriages that have floundered with the partners echoing those very words.

PAULINE. But Jane we haven't.

JANE (*beaming sympathy*). Haven't you?

PAULINE (*a little worried*). I don't think so.

JANE. You mean to tell me that there's been nothing strange about Dennis's behaviour. Nothing a little, out of the ordinary?

PAULINE. Well he, he . . . but it can't be anything to do with sex.

JANE. You let me be the judge of that. Now I want you to tell me everything.

PAULINE. Well . . . he has been behaving . . . strangely.

JANE. How do you mean?

PAULINE. For example he's been . . . well he's been teaching John filthy language.

JANE. John? His own son?

PAULINE. And . . . and he keeps something, in the bureau, and he says it's his poetry . . . but I know it's not. It's something else.

JANE. What?

PAULINE. Jane, I don't know.

JANE. Then why don't you look.

PAULINE. He keeps it locked. He won't let me have the key.

JANE (*staring at the offending bureau*). But this is preposterous.

PAULINE. I know.

JANE (*moving towards the bureau and eyeing it*). This cannot be allowed to continue. (*Pointing.*) In there. You mean there's something in there?

PAULINE. Yes.

JANE. Right. Let's have it open.

PAULINE. But Jane, Dennis keeps the key in . . .

JANE. Do you have a crowbar?

PAULINE. Oh Jane, I couldn't . . .

JANE. Pauline, this is not allowed. In a marriage the only secrets are murky secrets. Fetch a crowbar.

PAULINE. Jane, Jane I can't . . .

JANE. But I can. Fetch me a crowbar.

PAULINE. But if the lock's forced Dennis will know and . . .

JANE (*raising her hands*). All right Pauline, all right. If you want to leave it then fine, fine. If you want to live in mystery then that's up to you but it's patently obvious that you are living with a pervert.

PAULINE. Oh Jane, no . . .

JANE. When men begin locking cupboards and drawers, then you mark my words, there's only one thing they can be hiding.

PAULINE (*alarmed*). What, what?

JANE. Pornography. Stand back.

 She goes into an expert kung fu stance.

PAULINE (*rushing forward to shield the bureau*). No, Jane.

JANE. Pauline, don't you understand what it is you're protecting?

PAULINE. Yes, a genuine Queen Anne bureau.

JANE. Reproduction Pauline, reproduction.

PAULINE. All right, genuine reproduction, but we can't just smash it open.

JANE. Pauline I give you my word there will be no splinters. One blow, that's all it needs, one blow, delivered with precision. The insides of that bureau are seething with filth, bulging with the unspeakable. Pauline, what's he been filling his mind with? And if he's not stopped now, what's to be next? I'll tell you what's next, flashing his privates in the shopping arcade, breathing heavily down telephone lines, dressing up in women's clothes. Underpants? I'll bet it's knickers! Dennis wears knickers doesn't he Pauline, silk knickers?

PAULINE. No, NO!

JANE. Then he's got nothing to hide. Stand back.

> PAULINE *moves to one side as* JANE *summons up all her power and lunges. She kung fu's the bureau which remains placidly upright as* JANE *screams with pain.* ROGER *appears from the kitchen and we notice that there is some smoke coming through.*

ROGER. Erm, I don't want to make a fuss but there's, erm, a smell of er . . . the dinner . . .

JANE. Roger! Get an axe.

ROGER. Er the cottage pie . . .

JANE. That is not cottage pie, it is hachis au parmentier . . .

ROGER. Yeh, well the hachis . . .

JANE. Roger, an axe.

ROGER. Look the . . .

JANE. ROGER!

ROGER. Ogh . . .

> *He exits through kitchen and into garden.*

PAULINE. Jane, let me have a look at your hand.

JANE. My hand's fine. Just one blow, one heavy blow.

PAULINE. Don't you really think it would be best if we just forgot about . . .

JANE. Never. He might think he's beaten me . . .

The telephone begins to ring. ROGER enters with a huge and heavy sledge hammer.

ROGER. I couldn't find an axe, would this . . .

JANE. Perfect.

The door chimes begin to play the 'William Tell Overture'.

PAULINE. Jane . . . no.

JANE *marches to the hammer.*

JANE. Right.

PAULINE *caught between the need to stop* JANE, *answer the phone or go to the door, chooses the phone.*

PAULINE *(into telephone).* Who is it? *(She looks at the receiver with alarm and begins to scream, she drops the telephone receiver.* JANE, *who is attempting to lift the hammer, turns to* PAULINE.) Jane . . . it's *(pointing at receiver)*. It's . . . the phone. It's . . . heavy breathing.

JANE *(pushing the hammer at* ROGER *and marching to the phone).* Give that to me. Pauline, answer the door. Roger. Get that bureau open.

ROGER. But the dinner's . . . *(He appeals to* PAULINE *as she passes him on her way to the hall.)* Pauline the cottage pie . . .

JANE. No, Dennis Cain, you can just stop that stupid breathing now. It doesn't impress me Cain. *(To* ROGER.) Roger. Hit it.

ROGER *(pointing at the bureau).* What the?

JANE. Get it open. Now. *(Back to phone.)* We're just about to open this bureau Dennis Cain . . . we know what's in there and your game's up. In a second or two it will be open and we will all see the depths to which your mind has sunk.

She sees ROGER *tentatively holding the hammer.*

Hit it Roger.

As JANE *returns to the telephone,* ROGER *reluctantly but obediently raises the hammer above his head.*

You need a psychiatrist and we're going to see to it . . .

There is a terrible scream from the hall which causes ROGER *to momentarily pause with the sledge hammer above his head. He loses control of the hammer and the weight of it pulls him backwards so that both hammer and* ROGER *land in the centre of the dining table which should collapse.* ROGER *scrambles to his feet whilst pointing out of the window, into the garden.*

ROGER. Out there . . . out there, there's someone out there.

JANE. Where?

ROGER. In the garden, with an aerosol spray . . .

PAULINE enters from the hallway, distraught and crying. She carries the severed heads of a number of garden gnomes which she displays.

PAULINE. Jane . . . Jane . . . dead, all dead . . .

PAULINE sinks to the floor and stares comatose at the gnomic cadavers.

JANE (*retrieving the hammer from the debris of the table and thrusting it into* ROGER's *hands*). Get them Roger, get out there and show them what you're made of.

ROGER. But supposin' it isn't only the Parnes kids . . .

JANE. The hammer . . . you've got the hammer.

She bundles him out and returns to the phone.

Now you had better listen to this – a man who can teach filth to his own child, a man who makes obscene phone calls to his own wife is obviously very ill indeed and is in need of medical attention . . . Don't put on that funny voice with me.

Unseen, DENNIS *enters. He stares at the chaos.*

I know it's you Cain and I also know that you're a pervert Dennis Cain. You can be helped Dennis but you have to give yourself up without a struggle. That way would be better for everyone.

DENNIS. OK, I surrender.

> *She double takes* DENNIS *and the phone, screams and drops the receiver. She rushes for the door and is passed by* ROGER *who enters dragging the hammer behind him.*

ROGER (*to his disappearing wife*). I tried love, God knows I tried. But . . . (*He turns to* DENNIS). Ten of them at least Den, tryin' to paint your lawn. Overpowered me.

DENNIS. Oh hello Dad.

ROGER (*smoke now billowing from the kitchen*). The dinner. (*He rushes out to the kitchen.*)

> ROGER *enters with a smoking casserole dish.*

ROGER. Cottage Pie A La Burnt To Buggery.

> DENNIS *kneels and begins trying to resuscitate the 'dead' gnomes.*
> *Curtain.*

ACT TWO

Sometime later the same evening. The venetian blind is drawn to cover the window.

PAULINE, DENNIS, JANE *and* ROGER *are sat at the dining table which is profusely littered with empty wine bottles and aluminium trays from a Chinese take-away restaraunt. As we open,* PAULINE *is beginning to tidy away.*

JANE. That was a wonderful meal, Pauline.

PAULINE. Yes, but I don't see how I can take the credit for the cooking at the Chinese take-away.

JANE. And neither can you be expected to take the blame for guests who can't get here on time and force you to leave a meal waiting and waiting in the oven.

ROGER. Don't worry chucks, we love Cantonese food, don't we?

JANE. We adore oriental food Pauline.

ROGER. Food from the East – y' can't beat it. It's subtle on the palate y' see; none of this English, cover-it-all-in-gravy touch. Canton Cuisine, I love it: barbecued spare ribs with chow mein, a portion of curry sauce an' chips – ecstasy.

DENNIS. Me Mum and Dad were in the Chinese chippy.

JANE. When you think about it we're so lucky aren't we? When you think of the boring food that the last generation had to put up with and you compare it with what's available to us – Chinese food, Greek and Italian, Indian food, isn't it marvellous?

DENNIS. I was quite surprised to see them there. They must have got hold of an AA Road Map.

JANE. It is marvellous isn't it, how we can take advantage of the many different cultures which exist in our country.

DENNIS. Me dad had been in the take-away for half an hour.

He had the poor Chinese feller demented, trying to get him to understand how to make spam fritters.

JANE. I do think we're richer by being able to absorb from all these other cultures.

DENNIS. It was a good thing I arrived when I did; I was just in time to stop me dad climbin' over the counter to show the poor feller how it was done.

JANE. Of course a lot of people try to resist these influences . . . but not me. You only have to step into our house to see that we willingly take from other cultures.

DENNIS. And there's me Mum on the other side of the poor feller trying to teach him how to make real mushy peas.

JANE. We often have incense burning in the house don't we Roger? And Roger's got an Indian Kaftan dressing gown. There's that African mobile in the hall and the two Malayan tom-tom drums by the chimney breast.

DENNIS. It sounds like the headquarters of the United Nations.

PAULINE. And you've got that picture of the little Mexican boy, with the tears, haven't you?

JANE. Not any more love. Our artistic taste has moved on a little since then. We've found that's the case with art, haven't we Roger? You find, you see Pauline, that as you grow more familiar with art, so you can begin to appreciate the deeper forms.

ROGER. We gave the little Mexican feller to me Mum. Ogh she loves him, doesn't she? She sits there for hours just lookin' at him, tears streamin' down her cheeks. She has the time of her life, sittin' there cryin' at the little Mexican lad.

JANE. We've got a Lowry on that wall now.

PAULINE. An original?

JANE. A print of an original, yes.

ROGER. He was a primitive y' know. Lowry.

PAULINE. Was he Roger?

JANE. I look at that picture and see all those little people streaming out from the mill, dead people, with dead lives, nothing left for them, none of them going anywhere. I look at them and I always think, how lucky we are.

DENNIS. Me dad wanted to know who was shriekin' down the phone at him.

JANE. When you discover art you open such wide fields for the mind to roam.

DENNIS. I said to me dad it was a party line. He said, 'Which one – the Nazi Party?'

PAULINE. Dennis, I think we've had quite enough of your parents for one night.

DENNIS. And they haven't even been here.

PAULINE. What was that you were saying Jane?

JANE. It's not only art is it? Just think of all the other things in our lives which make us so much richer than those who went before.

PAULINE. I know. I don't know where I'd be without my Tupperware.

DENNIS. I think there's something very ominous about Tupperware. How can anyone make a multi-million pound business out of lids that don't fit properly?

PAULINE. There's nothing wrong with the lids. It's the people who put them on.

ROGER. Tupperware? It's incredible stuff. They were tellin' us, weren't they love, at the Convention, about this woman who bought one of their salad storers. Anyway, one day she goes down to the shops an' she buys this big bunch of celery an' she puts it in this salad storer. Anyway, next day, before she could eat it, she dropped dead, suddenly. She lived on her own like an' no-one knew she was dead for months an' months. But when they finally broke into her house, do you know what they found? That celery was still as fresh as a daisy. Now that's a recommendation isn't it?

DENNIS. What about all the people who lived around her?

ROGER. Oh, they all got salad storers after that.

DENNIS. I hate Tupperware.

PAULINE. We've had enough of your pet hates Dennis.

DENNIS. Every time I see a new piece of Tupperware in the house it feels like another little invasion has taken place . . . It seems to have a will of its own. I dreamt about it the other night. I dreamed that all the Tupperware in the house gelled together into one big plastic mass and began rollin' and slidin' up the stairs, on and on, through the bedroom door and sliding across the carpet, creepin' up onto the bed and pouncin' on me. The more I struggled, the more wrapped up in it I became until finally I stopped struggling and became The Tupperware Man.

JANE. They do say don't they that the most boring thing in the world is another person's dream.

DENNIS. An' in the next part of the dream I was Tupperware Man himself – I could fly and everything I touched turned to Tupperware. The world was in a panic. They sent Superman after me, and Batman and Robin and Luke Skywalker and Wonder Woman. But they were all helpless in the face of Tupperware Man. I turned them all into Tupperware – Batman and Robin became a butterdish an' egg cup, Superman was turned into a picnic box, Luke Skywalker into a salad spinner an' I turned Wonder Woman into a huge, tit-shaped jelly mould. Planet Earth was in danger of becoming a Tupperware Globe when the Americans came up with a new invention – Tupperware Woman. They sent her after me and I tried to resist, but it was no good, I was helpless in the face of her. An irresistible force drew me towards her, I couldn't stop myself, I struggled to keep away from her but I was drawn on and on. Beaten, I gave up, I kissed her and me lid flew off. It was all over.

PAULINE. I just pray he'll be all right after the holiday.

ROGER. 'Ey, it won't be long now will it?

He begins to sing 'The Birdy Song'. JANE *and* PAULINE *join in with accompanying routine.* DENNIS *is horrified.*

Great, remember it kid, remember?

DENNIS (*unenthusiastic*). Yeh, I do Rodge.

ROGER. The Fantastic Flamencos at Pepi's Night Spot.

DENNIS. Yeh, the Fantastic Flamencos.

ROGER. An' the Space Invaders at the hotel. I bet I thrash y' again this year Dennis.

DENNIS. Yeh. The space invaders.

ROGER. An' Sancho at the beach. He always remembers us dosen't he? He always makes sure we get a spot on the sand. Buenos notches Señor Roger. Never forgets us.

DENNIS. Why don't we go somewhere else this year?

PAULINE. But Dennis, we've booked for Spain.

DENNIS. Well let's unbook. Let's go somewhere else. Let's go to . . . to . . . India.

PAULINE. Dennis, I don't think you'd like India.

DENNIS. But I've never been.

JANE. I don't think India's a country I'd like to spend too much time in. Dennis.

DENNIS. Why? You're always burning incense an' he's got an Indian Kaftan dressing gown.

JANE. Yes but that's different.

DENNIS. Why is it?

JANE. And anyway that was before we saw Jewel In The Crown.

DENNIS. All right not India. But why not Japan or China. Yeh, China, we could all eat Chinese food till it was comin' out of our ears then.

PAULINE. I just know I wouldn't like Chinese food in China. It's different there.

ROGER. They don't have curry in Chinese chippies in China y' know?

PAULINE. Anyway Dennis, everyone wants to go to Spain.

DENNIS (*standing*). I don't.

PAULINE. Who'd like coffee?

DENNIS. Everybody hates Spain.

JANE. It is fresh coffee is it love?

DENNIS. Even the Spaniards hate Spain.

PAULINE. Fresh coffee in a bag, yes.

DENNIS. That's why the drink's so cheap. You have to be
constantly pissed to live there.

JANE. That's fine love. I just can't take instant coffee. My
stomach reacts against it.

DENNIS. You mean it makes you fart?

PAULINE. Take no notice of him Jane.

JANE. I'm not going to my love.

DENNIS. And I am not going to Spain.

PAULINE. Milk or cream Jane?

DENNIS. I was a youth once. I was young.

JANE. Do you have any skimmed milk Pauline? The cholesterol
content of milk ordinaire is enormous.

DENNIS. And now (*looking at his watch.*) I am forty. (*He goes up
to* JANE *and sticks his face into hers.*) Forty, forty, forty.

JANE (*standing*). Roger, will you do something about this please?

DENNIS. Forty years of age.

JANE. ROGER!

DENNIS (*shouting*). Forty years old today.

JANE. Roger will you do what must be done?

ROGER. All right, all right.

DENNIS. Forty, four O, forty forty . . .

ROGER (*arms raised*). OK kid. OK. (*Sings.*) Happy Birthday to
you, Happy Birthday to you. Happy Birthday dear Dennis,
Happy Birthday to you.

> *During the singing* JANE *and* PAULINE *hurriedly exit to the
> kitchen.* ROGER *grabs a gift wrapped parcel from the table.*

Here kid, you might as will open this now. It's from Val next door.

DENNIS *rips off the paper with a vengeance to reveal a compact disc.* ROGER *is beaming over his shoulder.*

Ogh, John Denver on compact disc. Fabulous kid, fabulous. Now you've got Denver on record, Denver on tape an' now Denver on CD.

DENNIS, *now maniacal, stares at him.*

Time for a toast eh?

As ROGER *heads for the wine bottle,* DENNIS *grabs the record-carrying case, goes to his record collection and begins to throw Denver records into the case. He rushes out through the kitchen and the back door.*

So here's to many more forties after this one kid and may every year be as happy as . . .

He turns to find himself addressing an empty room. PAULINE *appears at kitchen doorway.*

PAULINE. Why is he taking his record case into the garden?

ROGER. Well . . . Maybe he's testin' it.

PAULINE *exits to the kitchen and* ROGER *peers out of the venetian blinds.*

He seems to be bendin' down an' doin' somethin . . . He's takin' his records out of the carrier . . . He's er . . . what's he doin' now. Ogh, he's takin' the discs out of the sleeves . . . Now what's he doin'? Bloody hell. Would y' believe that? He's glidin' his records . . . Ogh . . . look at that one go . . . Right over the back roof. Ogh it didn't half go that one, look at that one, fabulous, fabulous . . .

JANE *and* PAULINE *enter.*

JANE. Roger will you please get out there and bring him in?

ROGER. Why? The kid's enjoyin' himself.

JANE. ROGER!

He goes.

PAULINE. Jane what am I going to do about him?

JANE. Just ignore him. Some men do anything to get attention.

PAULINE. But surely not gliding LP records?

JANE. You'd be surprised my love. (*Peeping through the blinds.*)
Roger . . . you're supposed to be bringing him in, not helping
him.

ROGER (*off*). I'm trying to gain his confidence.

Whoops of joy are heard offstage.

PAULINE. Will Roger be all right out there? Dennis can be very
stubborn you know.

JANE. Don't worry about Roger. The Duke Of Edinburgh did not
present Roger with his Award for nothing.

PAULINE. What am I going to do?

JANE. Pauline it's nothing. What's a nervous breakdown these
days?

PAULINE. A nervous breakdown?

JANE. The doctors will have him sorted out in no time. A little
electrical treatment. It could do Dennis a lot of good.

PAULINE. I feel sick.

JANE. Come on, I think you should have a little lie down. Let
Roger deal with this. Now come on, let's wash away those
tears. Never lose your composure Pauline.

*They exit as DENNIS and ROGER enter and head straight for
the record rack.*

DENNIS (*pulling out albums*). Neil Diamond.

ROGER (*taking the record*). Neil Diamond. He'll go far.

DENNIS. Wings.

ROGER. Ogh, we'll reach the far side of the estate with them.

DENNIS. Come on.

Telephone rings. DENNIS *answers.*

Sod off Dad – (*To* ROGER.) It's for you.

ROGER. Who the bloody hell . . .

DENNIS. The kids.

ROGER (*into the phone as* DENNIS *amasses more records*). Hello Amanda? Yes. . . . Yeah . . . But there's a fence . . . OK. Right. Tarar. I'll be there in two minutes.

DENNIS. Right let's go.

ROGER (*blocking him*). Don't you bloody move an inch.

DENNIS. What's up?

ROGER. I'll tell you what's up. Michael an' Amanda, an' your John are sittin in our lounge watchin' the video, when they heard a crash from the garden, followed by another one, and another. Dennis, me, you and John Denver have just razed my greenhouse to the ground.

> JANE *has appeared at the hall doorway and heard the news.*
> ROGER *rushes past her and out.* JANE *enters the room.*
> DENNIS *watches as she pours herself a large glass of wine.*

DENNIS. Well. I suppose you were insured.

JANE. I doubt it Dennis. Not against John Denver records anyway.

DENNIS. Well I'll erm . . .

JANE. Right Dennis, I want the truth. Is it premature ejaculation?

DENNIS (*astounded*). Pardon?

JANE. There's nothing to be embarrassed about Dennis. You musn't be shy. You must understand that we have to isolate the cause.

DENNIS. The cause of what?

JANE. The cause of gliding long playing records away, the cause of your refusal to participate on this estate, the cause of you being a somewhat solitary figure, a loner. Why, we ask ourselves, why doesn't Dennis join the weight watchers, the badminton club, the jogging circle? You're despised because of it you know Dennis. Yes, despised. But I say we have to try to

understand, to understand even that which we find obnoxious.
And to understand we have to isolate the cause. What is the
cause Dennis? Why don't you play badminton, why don't you
jog? Afraid of showering with the other men afterwards, is that
it? Have you got something to hide Dennis, or is your problem
the fact that you've got very little to hide?

DENNIS. You what?

JANE. Is that it Dennis? Do you lie awake at night, fretting,
wishing that you had been blessed with larger equipment?
Dennis, there's nothing to worry about. You're just a victim of
the myth that says bigger is better. Dennis that is a fallacy. If
only you'd read the right literature you'd understand that size,
in these matters, is of no consequence. Dennis, I can see that
this problem is wrecking your life. You've made it into an
enormous problem.

DENNIS. I thought it was more of a tiny problem.

JANE. You see Dennis, you turn a serious discussion into
something cheap and juvenile.

DENNIS. Jane I don't know where you've got this idea that I'm
going off my brains because I've got a little dick but the fact of
the matter is that I'm very happy with my dick and not having
sought the opportunity to compare its size with that of other
fellers I don't know whether it's economy, two star or premium
plus and I don't really care because I'm quite content with it
but as you seem to know far more than me in these matters and
no doubt have a wide range of experience from which to make
comparisons perhaps you'd like to pass expert judgement. Here,
have a look for yourself.

During the speech, DENNIS *has put his hand down his trousers
so that he protrudes a finger through his flies as though it were his
'dick'. It is this that* JANE *sees when she wheels round.*

JANE. Put that away (*backing away*). Don't bring that near me.
You flasher, I was right. Roger! Put it away, put it away.

DENNIS (*calm*). Jane . . . Jane.

*As she looks he removes his finger and she realises. He takes her
glass from her hand and pours a drink for both of them.*

Jane, I don't know where you get the idea that I'm sufferin' from things like premature ejaculation. If I have got a problem . . . it's got far more to do with going than coming.

JANE. Going? Going where? (DENNIS *takes her glass and refills it.*) Dennis I think I've had quite enough.

DENNIS. Drink it. It might keep you quiet for a minute.

JANE. I don't have to put up . . .

DENNIS. I'm gonna tell you a secret.

JANE. Oh.

DENNIS. Jane, do you know what's beneath the tiles of the kitchen floor?

JANE (*wide eyed*). What?

DENNIS. A tunnel. For the past couple of years I've been secretly trying to tunnel out of Castlehills.

JANE. Dennis . . .

DENNIS. No. Listen. I've been slowly, secretly digging, trying to tunnel beyond the boundaries, but whenever I finish the tunnel and break through the earth I always look out to find that the bungalows still stretch far beyond me. No matter how far the tunnel goes I never get clear of the boundary. I know there's a world out there – a world beyond zoned heating an' double glazed conservatories an' Radio Two and weight watchers and Richard fucking Clayderman, but I just can't reach it. Y' see, Castlehills is expanding faster than I can tunnel.

JANE (*looks at him*). Forget it Dennis.

DENNIS. I think I'm gonna have to change me tactics. The tunnel won't work. I'm gonna have to walk out of the gate.

JANE. Dennis, Dennis, you can't walk out of anywhere.

DENNIS. I can. It's dead easy. I just pack me things and walk away.

JANE (*she looks at him, smiles and shakes her head*). If it was that easy . . .

DENNIS. I can do it, I can.

JANE. Then why are you sitting here?

DENNIS. What? I'm gonna do it. I am.

JANE. When?

DENNIS. When? (*Bravely*.) Tonight. That's when. Tonight. I'll be off, into the night, down the long and lonesome road.

JANE. The A6?

DENNIS. The A6, the M6, Route 66, it doesn't matter as long as it's a road.

JANE. You won't do it Dennis.

DENNIS. See, if I stay I'll have to give in. Just like you've given in.

JANE. And what's that supposed to mean?

DENNIS. See, it's true Jane. Look at you. I remember when you were young. God it's difficult to remember now but yeh, you were young once and you had dreams like we all did, didn't you? You used to wear faded jeans all the time. Yeh, I remember now. What happened? You had long hair and slim hips and wide wide hopes for the future. I'll bet you don't even remember that do you? But I do. You used to laugh a lot, and joke and sing. Christ, everyone I knew used to fancy you. What happened?

JANE. Dennis, I was never like that.

DENNIS. You were you know. You were. Anyway, I've got no more time to talk, I've got to get packed.

JANE (*as DENNIS exits to hall*). I was never like that Dennis Cain. It must be someone else you're thinking of.

DENNIS (*entering from hall with rucksack*). OK.

JANE (*pause*). I was like that wasn't I?

DENNIS. Make up your mind.

JANE. I was. There was a time . . . a time when if I'd looked into the future and seen what I now am I would have . . . have . . . But what do you do? What else do you do?

DENNIS. You can get out. It's dead easy. Look, I'm going. I

know I can do it and once I realised that, it was like, like I was eighteen again and the world was in front of me again an' no longer behind me. Everythin' was open and available.

ROGER *enters.*

ROGER. Not a pane left. Not one pane left. Well he'll have to pay for it. Tell him he'll have to pay for it.

JANE. Tell him yourself.

JANE *exits.*

DENNIS. What's up Rodge? It's only a greenhouse.

ROGER. Was Dennis, was.

DENNIS. All right, was.

ROGER. Now listen kid, I want to talk to you. Your actions are beginnin' to give me cause for concern. You need a talkin' to lad. I'm going to ask you a few questions Dennis. And I want you to answer them honestly, right?

DENNIS. Go on, go on.

ROGER. Now . . . at this present time kid, do you feel . . . pretty . . . pissed off with life around here?

DENNIS. However did you guess Rodge?

ROGER (*nodding*). Yeh, yeh, I can see it. An' y' feel that the life you're livin' is pretty, how shall we say, empty? Yeh?

DENNIS *nods.*

Mm. An' you sometimes look at younger people an' think I wish I was their age.

DENNIS. Sometimes. Yeh.

ROGER. Mm. I thought so. I'll bet you've even become a little dissatisfied with Pauline, haven't y'?

DENNIS. To tell you the truth Rodge, I mean it's not that she's . . .

DENNIS. No, no, let me kid, let me. You see, I'll bet I know more about this than you. I'll bet, for example, you've even started to hate people haven't y'?

DENNIS. I have.

ROGER. Even people close to you, people you love. Dennis, if I'm not mistaken I'll bet you even hate me an' Jane at the moment.

DENNIS. Rodge you wouldn't believe how much I hate you and Jane.

ROGER. It's all right kid, it's all right . . . I think I would.

DENNIS. I don't think you would Rodge.

ROGER. Now look here kid, if I say I realise how much you hate us, then I do. But I want you to realise right away that hatred like that is perfectly normal. Look pal, you're not revealing anythin' new to me y' know. Dennis the symptoms you've just described to me are the classic symptoms of 'humpwish'.

DENNIS. Hump what?

ROGER. Humpwish.

DENNIS. What do I do about it?

ROGER. Easy. Instead of sittin' around wishin', you get out an' start humpin'. A few afternoons off work, spent between the sheets in someone else's bungalow an' you'll be a new man. What you need is an affair.

DENNIS. But I don't want an affair.

ROGER. Of course you do. There's not a feller I see who doesn't have somethin' on the side. They're all at it on this estate. It's like a rabbit warren. Why do you think there's so much subsidence round here? A feller needs an antidote to his frustration. You know I've got one or two on the go, don't y'? All these clubs an' committees I'm associated with, you don't think it's 'cause of the good of me health do y'? There's Big Wendy at the Weight Watchers. Pam, y' know Pam at the tennis club, been goin' on for some years that has. Glenda, from the parent/teachers, Carol from the ramblers' club, Mrs Clegg the lollipop lady. Y' can't beat it man. Get out there an' put it about.

DENNIS. It seems to me there's nowhere left to put it.

ROGER. There's plenty more out there Dennis.

DENNIS. But none that I fancy Rodge.

ROGER. Don't be soft, there must be.

DENNIS. Well, I suppose . . . I suppose there is one I've always fancied havin' a crack at.

ROGER. Well you get stuck in there an' nip these dangerous feelings in the bud.

DENNIS. Yeh, I only realised it tonight but . . .

ROGER. Don't waste a second, get movin' an' get stuck in.

DENNIS. Yeh, I've always fancied Jane.

ROGER (*still under his own momentum*). This estate, it's full of . . . What? What did you say? I am warning you Cain, here and now I am warning you. That woman is the mother of my children. You keep your distance. Where's your sense of morality?

DENNIS. Mine? Don't worry Rodge. I wouldn' go near Jane.

ROGER. An' you better bloody hadn't.

DENNIS. Honest. I wouldn't do anything with Jane. I wouldn't touch her.

ROGER. What d' y' mean? I'll have you know my wife is a very desirable woman.

DENNIS. I know that. But that's not what I want Rodge. When I was on that slip road today I should have done it. I should have gone, disappeared forever.

ROGER. So why didn't y'?

DENNIS. I told y'. I had the car with me.

ROGER. Well you could've dumped the car. Left it.

DENNIS. I thought of that. But the weekend shoppin' was in the boot. I mean, I couldn't leave those left behind to starve, could I? I know now though Rodge, I know there's no other way out. I can see that clearly, after tonight. I'm not a domestic pet Rodge. I'm not like you and the rest of them round here. I'm a wild beast, not a cat who's had his bollocks trimmed. I'm a roamer Rodge, Bob Dylan speaks plainly to me. I'm a wanderer and a gypsy and a poet.

ROGER. A poet? You?

DENNIS. Yeh, me. (*Hands him a cigarette packet.*) Read that.

ROGER (*reads*). Government Health Warning. Smoking Can . . .

>   DENNIS *turns the paper over for him.*

In the land of proud vasectomies
Where cholesterol's more talked of than weather
They've Black and Deckered their hopes
Deep-frozen their dreams forever.
In the country of Mothercare Angels
Where Tupperware rules OK
They're counting the special offers
They harvested through the day.
In a place called 'dead forever'
On the banks of a man-made mere
The only song the natives sing
Is 'Christ Get Me Out Of Here'.

Not bad kid . . . not bad . . .

DENNIS. I'm goin' Rodge.

ROGER. Goin'? Goin' where?

DENNIS. Away, off into the night. Just me, a lone figure at the
side of the road, an outline in the truckers' lights, the traveller,
the outsider, the one who had the courage to do it.

ROGER. Come off it. You're not goin' anywhere an' you know it.

DENNIS. You won't say that when I'm gone.

ROGER. Gone? Don't be soft. Even if you were serious and you
did go, have you thought what it would be like? Eh? What
would you be doin' eh? While we'd be here sleepin' under warm
continental quilts, you'd be out there kippin' in the grass or on
the sand. While we'd be at good tables, eating good food you'd
be sittin' round some bloody camp fire. While we'd be comin'
home every night to the same wife an' the same house there
wouldn't be the same security for you. You wouldn't have
responsibilities. Life would just be an endless list of different

places an' new encounters an' fresh women. Christ, you lucky bugger. I'll get us a beer.

DENNIS *laughs.*

ROGER *goes into the kitchen and closes the door behind him.* JANE *enters from the hall door.*

JANE. Dennis. Take me with you.

DENNIS (*turning from his packing*). Now Jane . . . Jane, just hold on Jane.

JANE. You're right Dennis, you've made me realise . . .

DENNIS. Jane . . . be careful.

JANE. I've had enough of being careful. I'm sick of being careful. You're right and I'm coming with you.

DENNIS. Jane, you can't. You've got two lovely kids and the most up-to-date fitted kitchen on the estate, now why jeopardise . . .

JANE. Sod my kitchen. Let him have it. The two of us. You and me on the road. Dennis, I'm going to get changed. I'm going to borrow a pair of your jeans.

She exits through hall door.

DENNIS. Jane . . . Jane . . . come back it's . . . Oh shit.

PAULINE *dressed in anorak and jeans enters from the hall.*

Oh shit.

PAULINE. Dennis, we're going away. I've decided that what you need is a rest. There's no point in waiting for a holiday. You could be in an institution before then. No, we'll get away now. To the Lake District. Plenty of walking and fresh air is much better than pills or electrical treatment for a man in your condition. We can collect John, he can sleep in the car, I've packed a few things and we can . . .

DENNIS (*shrieking*). No, no, no, no.

PAULINE. Dennis, don't shout. I know you're not well but at least have some consideration for . . .

DENNIS. I am not going anywhere in the car. I am going on the road. (*Raises his thumb.*)

PAULINE. Hitch-hiking? Oh that'll be fine won't it? And supposing we don't get a lift?

DENNIS. Not we, me. I am not going to the Lake District. I am not going to Spain. I am going to the slip road and going to wherever the lifts happen to take me. Apart from Spain that is. If I'm unlucky enough to pick up a truck going to Spain I'll just get off at France.

PAULINE. Dennis. Is this really what you feel you must do?

DENNIS. Yes. Yes.

PAULINE (*considers*). All right Dennis. If that's what you feel you must do then that's what we'll do. If your health depends on . . .

DENNIS. Pauline, I am not talking about a week, a couple of weeks, a month. I want to go for good.

PAULINE. What?

DENNIS. Forever.

PAULINE. Leaving everything we've built up?

DENNIS. Yes, yes. You can have it all.

PAULINE. What do you mean?

DENNIS. I mean I'm going alone. OK. There I've said it. I am going alone.

PAULINE. Oh no you're not. Not in the state you're in. I'm coming with you.

DENNIS. Look, Pauline, listen. I'm talking about going on the road, forever – a wanderer, a freak of the highway. It's rough out there. It's hard an' it's heavy an' it's lawless – Pauline have you seen the M6?

PAULINE. Yes, and that's why you need your family to look after you.

DENNIS. Pauline, I'm not a domestic pet.

PAULINE. Now there's a drop of milk in the fridge. We might as well take a flask with us.

DENNIS (*as she exits to the kitchen*). No . . . No . . .

> *He goes to follow her but is stopped by the appearance of*
> ROGER, *well pissed, clutching a half finished bottle of wine and*
> *wearing anorak and wellingtons.*

ROGER. Kid . . . I'm' coming with y'.

> PAULINE *enters from the kitchen, clutching a flask as* JANE
> *enters wearing a pair of* DENNIS's *jeans.*

PAULINE. Come on Dennis.

JANE. Dennis let's go.

> DENNIS *looks at the three of them before sinking onto the settee.*
> *The three of them see each other.*

PAULINE. What's going on?

ROGER. What are you doin' in Dennis's trousers?

JANE (*defiant*). I'm going away with Dennis.

ROGER. You're not. Dennis is comin' away with me.

PAULINE. Dennis will you please tell these people that you are
coming away with your wife and your child?

ROGER. He's comin' with me.

JANE. Come on Dennis. I'm ready.

DENNIS (*sighing*). I'll tell you what – you lot go an' I'll stay here.
What's the point anyway? It seems everyone's goin'. Right this
minute you probably can't get onto the slip road for the queues
of hitch-hikers.

ROGER. You? Goin' away with Dennis? You can't go anywhere.
You've got your children to look after.

JANE. You look after them.

ROGER. Me? Me, how the hell can I look after them? I hardly
know them.

JANE. Yes. You look after them. You try living your life with two
kids in a flea-sized dormer bungalow. You try it, because I
won't be there. I'm going away with Dennis. Go on Roger . . .
fuck off.

PAULINE/ROGER. Jane!

JANE. What's wrong? Can't you cope with a little real language, an occasional salty phrase or two. That's how he (*Referring to* DENNIS.) talks. He understands. He's real.

DENNIS. Oh buggery.

JANE. Yes Dennis, that's it. Real language. Me and Dennis, we're going out on the road. I've had enough of the rest of you. But I don't have to put up with it anymore, I don't have to pretend anymore, look . . . I'm on my own . . . I'm wild . . . I'm free. I'll tell them . . . all of them . . .

> *She rushes to the window, half pulls up the blind and begins to shriek out of the open window.*

Fuck, fuck, fuck, fuck, fuck, fuck . . . Can you hear me Val? Fuck fuck fuck . . .

> ROGER *tries to wrestle her away from the window but with a perfectly aimed elbow she downs him.*

Get off me. Get off.

ROGER. You can't do this. What about me?

JANE. You? You. You can get one of your other little Phase Two wives to look after you.

ROGER. What love?

JANE. What love? Do you think I'm blind? I know Roger. I've known for ages, about all of them, all the other women.

ROGER. All of them?

JANE. Pam at the tennis club . . . Glenda from the PTA . . . Carol from the Ramblers . . .

DENNIS. Wendy from the Weight Watchers.

JANE. Yes, yes, yes.

ROGER. Bloody hell. (*Tentatively testing her.*) Mrs Clegg?

JANE. I know about them all Roger.

ROGER. An' it doesn't matter?

JANE. None of them matter Roger . . . because you don't matter.

ROGER. Oh. (*Pause. Suddenly.*) What about Mavis at work?

JANE. Tch. And Val from next door?

DENNIS. Val? Bloody hell?

ROGER. Belinda? Dianne?

JANE. Yes, yes.

ROGER. Tracey?

JANE (*bored*). Yes.

ROGER. Susan . . .

JANE. From, the supermarket, yes, yes, yes.

PAULINE (*who has been comforting* ROGER. *Suddenly*). And
    Pauline, from The Haven. Tell them Roger . . . Yes me . . .
    Pauline.

   DENNIS *turns in slow amazement.* JANE *takes a step forward.*

JANE (*horrified*). Pardon?

DENNIS (*in disbelief*). You? And him?

PAULINE. Yes! Me and Roger. Me and boring old Roger.

ROGER. Boring?

PAULINE. Yes. A lot of the time. But never on Wednesday
    afternoons. On Wednesday afternoons it's good. It's very good,
    isn't it Roger? Because Roger can be very imaginative . . .

DENNIS. Oh spare us the details . . .

PAULINE. He's so imaginative that on Wednesday afternoons
    he's not Roger. Tell them Roger, tell them who you are on
    Wednesday afternoons . . . tell them who you are for me . . .

ROGER (*sheepish*). John Denver.

DENNIS. Ogh . . . this is disgustin'.

PAULINE. Tell them who I am Roger.

ROGER. No . . . no.

PAULINE. On Wednesday afternoons, I am Joan Bakewell.

JANE (*moving towards* ROGER). I'll kill you . . . You bastard . . .
    I am Joan Bakewell . . . I am . . .

ROGER. Oh love, I'm sorry . . . I tried to persuade her to be someone else but she wouldn't. She had a try at bein' Selina Scott but it didn't work for us.

JANE (*in tears*). I am Joan Bakewell.

PAULINE (*jubilant*). No . . . I am. And I am wonderful as Joan Bakewell . . . I am glorious . . . Tell her Roger, go on, tell her what I am on Wednesday afternoons. Tell her . . .

ROGER (*hopeless gesture*). She's my . . . my Bakewell tart.

JANE *suddenly shrieks and goes into a karate stance.* PAULINE *moves to protect* ROGER. DENNIS *slowly begins to smile and then to laugh until it becomes uncontrollable, convulsive, as* JANE *tries to lay one on* ROGER *who manages to keep avoiding the aimed blows. Finally* ROGER *and* PAULINE *have their backs against the bureau.* JANE *lets fly with a stunning karate chop and* PAULINE *and* ROGER *fling themselves aside.* JANE *connects with the bureau, the one mammoth blow smashing it into a thousand pieces. Aerosol cans pour forth relentlessly, filling the room. The three of them, stunned, turning and looking at* DENNIS.

JANE. You?

DENNIS (*wild, maniacal, leaping up onto settee*). Yes, me me me. I did it . . . all of it. (*He arms himself with an aerosol can.*) But don't worry . . . I am going . . . and going alone . . . You lot?

ROGER. He's mad, he's bloody mad.

DENNIS. You lot stay here an' get on with your fornication. I'm not goin' anywhere with any of you. You? If we ended up in the desert you'd organise it; you'd stop the sands from shiftin' an' have the nomads holdin' Tupperware parties . . . Mad, mad, mad . . .

He begins spraying the aerosol, sending JANE *and* PAULINE *rushing for the cover of the hall and* ROGER *out into the kitchen.*

He turns and begins to spray his name onto the venetian blind.

I'm going . . . alone . . .
I can do it . . .
I know I can . . .

JANE (*off*). Roger . . . are you safe?

ROGER (*off*). I'm in the kitchen.

JANE (*off*). Roger . . . we'll have to bring him under control

ROGER. He's mad, you realise that? He's bloody mad.

JANE. I think we all realise that now Roger . . . That's why I was pretending to go away with him. He had to be humoured Roger . . . Now we have to bring him under control.

ROGER. He's armed y' know.

JANE. We are aware of that Roger. But we too can arm ourselves. Arm yourself man, arm yourself . . . We've got to bring him under control.

> ROGER *enters, wary, tentative, hands concealed behind his back.* DENNIS, *who has completed painting his name wheels, aerosol at the ready.*

DENNIS. Move Rodge. I don't want to but if I have to . . .

ROGER. It's not as simple as that kid. You see I'm armed as well.

> *From behind his back he reveals a plastic bottle of washing-up liquid and one of liquid Ajax.*

DENNIS. Are you gonna get out of the way or do I have to let you have it?

ROGER. You always wanted to be some kind of bloody hero – didn't y' Dennis? But somone forgot to tell you pal – it's not the nineteen sixties anymore. These days, there's no place for your kind of hero.

DENNIS. Just move Rodge . . .

ROGER. It's the nineteen eighties Dennis – an' you know who the real heroes are today. Us. Us lot who get on with it quietly without whingin' an' whinin'. Us lot who mow our lawns and build our conservatories an' listen to Jimmy Young . . .

> DENNIS *laughs.*

Oh yes you can laugh kid.

> *Unseen by* DENNIS, JANE *and* PAULINE *enter from the hall.*

JANE *carries a vacuum cleaner tube and* PAULINE *carries the sleeping bag from* DENNIS's *rucksack. They creep up behind him.*

DENNIS. You're not gonna stop me Rodge, I mean it. None of you are gonna stop me. I'm goin' . . .

PAULINE *slips the sleeping bag over his head. It is swiftly pulled down as* JANE *binds his arms with the vacuum cleaner tubing.*

JANE. We've got him . . . it's all right . . . everybody's safe, he's harmless now.

PAULINE. Dennis how could you?

ROGER. What do we do now?

PAULINE. What are you doing Roger?

ROGER. Phoning the bloody police –

PAULINE. No . . . No . . . Not the police . . .

ROGER. Not the police? There's a lot of people round here want the responsible party brought to justice . . .

JANE (*relieving him of the telephone*). Roger . . . you don't mean bring the police for Dennis do you?

ROGER. Of course I do.

JANE. But Dennis hasn't done anything. Have you Dennis?

Muffled cries from the sleeping bagged figure on the settee.

Of course you haven't Dennis. He might think he was responsible, but that's all it is – thought, mistaken thought. How could Dennis have committed these recent outrages? He's one of us Roger . . . for all his little failings he's one of us and will be seen as one of us. If Dennis was seen to commit crimes in the community then those crimes would, I'm sad to say, reflect upon us, all of us.

ROGER. Oh.

DENNIS (*Muffled*). It was me. I did it.

JANE. Of course you didn't Dennis, you're deluding yourself. Dennis you couldn't have done it . . . because we wouldn't believe you.

ROGER (*pointing at venetian blind*). What about that?

JANE (*in one pull of a cord she reverses the blind thereby eliminating DENNIS's name*). What? I can't see anything.

PAULINE. So what are we going to do Jane?

JANE. What we are going to do Pauline is understand. Dennis wants to go away. Well perhaps he's right. Perhaps we are, all of us, a little tired of doing what is expected all the time. But, you see Dennis's problem is that he doesn't understand how to organise these things. It's simple really, with a little planning. We've all got a month's holiday haven't we? So, why don't we go on the road?

ROGER. Hitch-hiking?

JANE. Roger! We buy a truck no . . . not a truck . . . an old bus . . . and we fix it up . . .

ROGER. Brilliant, an' we all go away in it?

Throughout the following, and as their enthusiasm for the venture builds we hear increased groans of dismay from the sleeping bag.

PAULINE. We fix it up as a holiday home.

JANE. Exactly.

ROGER. Like Cliff Richard in Summer Holiday.

Terrible moans from the sleeping bag.

PAULINE. Oh it could be lovely.

ROGER. It's a great idea.

JANE. We drop out . . . for a month.

ROGER. All of us . . . in our own bus.

JANE. Why not? After all we're almost one big happy family aren't we?

Throughout the above DENNIS has managed to get up and unseen by the others has got himself out of the door.

PAULINE. Oh Jane. (*Laughs.*) Surely you don't think . . . I mean you do realise that what I said about Roger and I was just a ploy . . . to bring Dennis out into the open. I was pretending

. . . like you were pretending . . . wasn't I Roger?

ROGER. Of course you were . . .

JANE. Pauline . . . of course I realised. The idea of you having
an affair. (*Laughs.*)

ROGER. So we club together, buy an old bus, right? It could be
fantastic y' know. We could do what we wanted with it . . . put
a cooker in . . . an' a fridge . . .

PAULINE. We could get a telly an' a video and partition a bit
off for the kids.

ROGER. Anything kidder, we could even pick up a second hand
dishwasher . . . We could stop where we wanted . . .

PAULINE. Go wherever we wanted, like gypsies.

JANE. Organised gypsies Pauline.

ROGER. It's a wonderful idea. What do you think Den . . .

He turns and sees that DENNIS *is no longer there.* PAULINE
rushes to the hall.

PAULINE. Dennis . . . Dennis . . . Dennis.

JANE (*to kitchen*). Dennis . . . Dennis.

PAULINE. He's gone . . . he's gone . . .

ROGER. He's gone. He's bloody done it.

JANE. Roger, the slip road, quickly.

As they rush out of the front door, DENNIS *enters from the
kitchen, pulling the sleeping bag off his head. He sees the empty
room. He notices the open front door. He stands, trying to will
himself through it.* JANE *rushes in, heading for the phone but
stops when she sees* DENNIS. *She stands for a moment and
watches him confronting the door. She holds the door wide open for
him.*

JANE. Go on Dennis, go on. There's nothing stopping you.

*She finally closes the door as it becomes obvious that he is not
going to go. She goes to the kitchen and reappears with a can of
lager. She opens it and hands it to him.*

Why not Dennis?

DENNIS (*shrugs*). I dunno. I just can't.

Pause.

Maybe . . . maybe I'll have another go next year . . . and maybe the year after that and the year after . . . Or maybe I'll just . . . (*Considers.*) What do you do on Wednesday afternoons Jane?

JANE. Not a lot. Why?

DENNIS. Fancy a visitor this Wednesday?

JANE. Who?

DENNIS. Me.

JANE. All right.

DENNIS. What time?

PAULINE (*off*). Jane – Jane –

JANE. He's here, Pauline, he's back. Two o'clock.

She exits through kitchen. DENNIS absently switches on the TV. We hear a snatch of John Denver singing. PAULINE enters.

PAULINE (*out of breath. She stands looking at him as he looks at the TV*). Dennis. I thought you'd gone.

DENNIS. Me? I'm not going anywhere.

She rushes to him and embraces him.

PAULINE. Go on. You sit down and watch the telly while I get this mess sorted out.

She begins tidying the room as DENNIS sits in front of the TV, sipping his lager. He changes channels and we hear an old movie soundtrack.

There is a loud knocking on the window. DENNIS gets up and crosses to the window. As he looks through the blinds we hear:

VOICE (*off*). Eh up son! It's a good job you put your name on the window – or we'd never 'ave bloody found it.

Blackout.